THE FOOD AND COOKING OF

BRAZIL

THE FOOD AND COOKING OF
BRAZIL

TRADITIONS • INGREDIENTS • TASTES • TECHNIQUES • 65 CLASSIC RECIPES

FERNANDO FARAH

AQUAMARINE

This edition is published by Aquamarine
an imprint of Anness Publishing Ltd
info@anness.com
www.annesspublishing.com

A CIP catalogue record for this book is available from the British Library.

Publisher: Joanna Lorenz
Editorial Director: Helen Sudell
Executive Editor: Joanne Rippin
Designer: Adelle Morris
Photography: Jon Whitaker
Food Stylist: Aya Nishimura
Prop Stylist: Liz Hippisley
Production: Ben Worley

COOK'S NOTES

Bracketed terms are intended for American readers.
For all recipes, quantities are given in both metric and imperial measures and, where appropriate, in standard cups and spoons. Follow one set of measures, but not a mixture, because they are not interchangeable.
Standard spoon and cup measures are level. 1 tsp = 5ml, 1 tbsp = 15ml, 1 cup = 250ml/8fl oz.
Australian standard tablespoons are 20ml. Australian readers should use 3 tsp in place of 1 tbsp for measuring small quantities.
American pints are 16fl oz/2 cups.
American readers should use 20fl oz/2.5 cups in place of 1 pint when measuring liquids.
Electric oven temperatures in this book are for conventional ovens. When using a fan oven, the temperature will probably need to be reduced by about 10–20°C/20–40°F. Since ovens vary, you should check with your manufacturer's instruction book for guidance.
The nutritional analysis given for each recipe is calculated per portion (i.e. serving or item), unless otherwise stated. If the recipe gives a range, such as Serves 4–6, then the analysis will be for the smaller portion size, i.e. 6 servings. The analysis does not include optional ingredients, such as salt added to taste.
Medium (US large) eggs are used unless otherwise stated.

Front cover image: Moqueca baiana, Fish stew in coconut milk (for the recipe see page 55).

PUBLISHER'S NOTE

Although the advice and information in this book are believed to be accurate and true at the time of going to press, neither the author nor the publisher can accept any legal responsibility or liability for any errors or omissions that may have been made nor for any inaccuracies nor for any loss, harm or injury that comes about from following instructions or advice in this book.

PICTURE ACKNOWLEDGEMENTS

Thanks to the following agencies for the use of their images: Alamy jacket front bottom 2nd left, pp3, 6b, 7b & tl, 9tl & b, 10b, 11t & br, 13tl, 14tl & b, 22, 45, 47, 83, 101; Corbis pp6t, 7tr, 8tl & tr, 9tr, 13tr, 15b & t; Getty jacket front bottom right and back bottom left, pp11bl, 12b, 14tr, 21, 63, 80, 99; istock 12t & m, 13bl.

Contents

Introduction

Brazil is a country of dazzling beauty, with a wide variety of different climates and ecosystems. With millions of kilometres of richly fertile land, a lush coastline, and some of the longest rivers in the world, Brazil has the means to supply itself with almost every kind of ingredient. The country is also home to a population of great ethnic and cultural diversity, whose heritage is expressed in vibrant art and festivals, and epitomized by a lavish love of Brazilian food.

A fertile land

The native population of Brazilian Indians had lived undisturbed for centuries when Brazil was discovered and claimed for Portugal by the navigator Pedro Alvares Cabral on 22 April 1500. Only a few days later, the Portuguese fleet's chronographer, Pero Vaz de Caminha, added this perceptive comment to his letter to the king of Portugal: 'In this land, whatever one plants will grow'.

The results of colonization

The history of most South American countries is scarred by wars between tribes or against invaders, but Brazil was very fortunate. Portugal's colonization generally had a benign effect – although this was not necessarily intentional. In the 16th century Portuguese explorers, like their descendants, were experienced traders in all types of spices and lucrative crops such as sugar cane, tobacco and coffee, which they quickly established in Brazil. Millions of African slaves were brought to Brazil to work on the plantations, and their food culture also made its way into farmhouse kitchens, to blend with the culinary traditions of native Brazilian Indians and their Portuguese masters.

Brazil's relatively gentle colonization process is reflected in the cuisine of the country, where many Portuguese and native recipes, such as Bacalhau à Gomes de Sá (salt cod and potatoes), for instance, or the Brazilian Tapioca Pancakes, still found in many cities throughout Brazil, remain unchanged. Other recipes have benefited from Brazilian ingredients – for example, the African recipe for Bobó de Camarão (prawn stew in a thick creamy sauce), in which the African breadfruit has been replaced with Brazilian cassava root – and the addition of coconut to many recipes.

Above: The dramatic Iguaçú Falls, in the Amazon rainforest.

Below: Christ the Redeemer, Rio.

Passion for life and food

For many Brazilians, their passion for life is expressed through family, food, the beach, carnival and football. Football is perhaps Brazil's second largest religion. Regardless of gender or age, all Brazilians support a local team and are immensely proud of their five-time FIFA World Cup – winning national team. Most ardent fans will gather before a game at bars and go to the stadium in groups then will promptly return to the bar to celebrate their victory, or drown their sorrows.

Above: Every year Rio hosts a carnival parade of the city's samba schools at the Sambódromo.

Right: The famous view of Sugarloaf Mountain, overlooking the bay and city of Rio de Janeiro, by night.

Below: The popular Boa Viagem beach in the city of Recife, in the north-east of Brazil. Ambulantes – food and drink vendors – walk up and down the beach all day, selling cashew nuts, raw oysters, fried shrimp, little portions of soup, and fresh fruit juices.

For most coastal dwellers, the beach is a gym, community centre, fashion show and cocktail party rolled into one. Foot-volley, surfing, jogging, racquetball and promenading up and down the water's edge, meeting friends and admiring each other's tanned bodies, are all popular activites fuelled by the large industry of mobile catering. Beach-front kiosks and hard-working street vendors battle to outdo each other, providing fresh coconut water, lemonade, iced tea, ice cream, cassava biscuits (cookies), fruit, sandwiches, grilled cheese sticks or coconut tapioca pudding.

In late February or early March, the whole country's attention turns to carnival – a four-day-long debauched celebration of music, dance, glamour, eating and drinking. Rio's carnivals may be world-famous, but there are parades and street parties in every town. Food is kept to light dishes with plenty of cold cuts and fresh fruit, and revellers are kept cool by consuming large amounts of freezing cold beer, batidas and caipirinhas.

A celebration of Brazilian food

This collection of authentic regional dishes are eaten and loved by cooks in city restaurants, rural farmhouses and private homes throughout Brazil. Choose a main course, pair it with cheese bread, and you have a simple supper, or go all-out and make a traditional Feijoada – the black bean and pork feast – and invite the entire family round for a splendid Brazilian celebration of life.

The Culinary History of Brazil

When the Portuguese sailor Pedro Álvares Cabral first set foot in Brazil in April 1500, he could not have imagined that he was merely the first in a long line of major influences on the culture of this newly discovered country. Brazilian cuisine combines the dishes of its native inhabitants with flavours from Portugal, Africa, the Middle East and East Asia, as immigrants have arrived from these countries over the centuries, bringing their food traditions with them.

Above: A house built in traditional colonial style on an old coffee plantation at Fazenda Campo Alto, São Paulo.

Above left: A native worker dries cassava pulp over a large, open pan. The resulting flour, 'farinha', can be stored for a long time and transported long distances. A lot of the farinha consumed in the south east comes from cooperatives of small farms in the north.

Brazil before the Portuguese

There is archaeological evidence that human beings lived in Brazil as far back as 60,000 years ago. Today it is estimated that when the Portuguese arrived, the native population numbered between 1 and 5 million. Now, after centuries of contact with colonizing forces, their numbers have been reduced to a few hundred thousand individuals.

Many tribes still live exactly as they did before the Portuguese came, and in most areas, eating habits remain unchanged. Fish is the main source of protein, but tribes also hunt for wild pigs and smaller forest animals. They eat a wide variety of fruits and nuts, and their main source of carbohydrates is the root of the cassava plant. Cassava, or manioc, is the only significant crop cultivated by the tribes and it is of great importance to their diet. Villages usually maintain three separate fields in different stages of growth, so that it can be harvested throughout the year. Ancient methods of extracting the cassava's starch are still used today. The remaining pulp is ground and dried to make flour.

Portuguese colonization

By 1560 the Portuguese had divided this massive country into several separate territories, appointed governors and installed a

Above left: A Bahian woman cooks traditional food in Salvador, Bahia state.

Above right: Indigenous children of the Waurá tribal community of Canarana, deep in the heart of the Brazilian rainforest.

central government. Now that the full potential of the fertile terrain was realized, the focus shifted from the extraction of natural products to the production of lucrative crops for export. Sugar and coffee plantations began to dominate the landscape in the east of Brazil.

The African influence

Between 1570 and 1888, over 3 million African slaves were brought to Brazil, first to labour on the plantations, and later to work in the mines digging for gold and precious stones. African women were often employed as domestic helpers and therefore influenced the food being prepared in the kitchens of the big farmhouses. Coconut milk and dendê (palm oil) were used to flavour dishes, and a variety of different peppers added heat and spice to blander Portuguese recipes. Adding a grain to sauces to make thicker pastes is another African invention, and in Brazil, cassava flour substituted the grains and yams the slaves had used. Tutu (black bean and cassava flour purée), pirão (fish stock and cassava flour purée) and Bobó de Camarão (prawns in cassava purée and coconut milk sauce) are typical examples of this new form of multicultural cooking.

Below: Beach kiosk on the beachfront promenade, Ponta Negra, Natal.

Modern immigration

After Brazil became independent in 1822, the country's ports were thrown open to 'all friendly nations'. A small number of immigrants started flowing into the country, but after the abolition of slavery 66 years later, a shortage of labour began to attract larger numbers of workers. The Swiss and Germans were the first to arrive, followed by the Italians and Spanish, all bound for the coffee plantations of the south-east. The 20th century saw an increase in the flow of Japanese and Middle Eastern immigrants.

Italians quickly popularized the use of pasta, and brought a variety of sausages and cured meats. Japanese immigrants adapted the Chinese spring roll into a delicate deep-fried pastry pocket called Pastel. hummus, sfiha, Kibe and other Lebanese dishes are now often sold by street vendors on the beach; and anyone drinking Brazilian wine should make a toast to the German immigrants who brought their wine-making skills with them.

Landscape and Climate

Brazil is the size of a continent. It is by some distance the largest country in South America, and the fifth largest country in the world. Its 26 states and one Federal District are grouped into five major regions with widely differing ecosystems and climates, from sizzling tropical heat and humidity near the Equator to the clear, cold air of the southern highlands. The climate and historic and social factors combine to influence the kinds of food produced and eaten in each region.

The Amazonian rainforest

The far north of Brazil is dominated by the rainforest and the mighty Amazon river, with its many tributaries. Northern cuisine makes full use of the special ingredients only found in the forest, which makes it hard to reproduce elsewhere. Typical dishes include pato ao tucupí (duck in tucupí broth) and tacacá, a soup sold by street vendors as a pick-me-up. Desserts include many tropical fruits that are difficult to find even in other Brazilian regions, although some have found their way to the export market – for example, brazil nuts and the nutritious berry, açaí.

The arid north-east

A large part of Brazil's north-eastern region is taken up by the Caatinga, an expanse of land as big as France and Spain put together. In this dry region there is usually a little rainfall in the summer, but hardly any in winter. In spite of the harsh conditions, about 15 million people live there. The climate is perfect for making carne seca (beef jerky, or dried beef) which is especially popular in the north-eastern tip of Brazil. Famous dishes include Jabá com Jerimum (beef jerky with pumpkin) and Escondidinho (beef and cassava pie).

Bahia, on the northeast Atlantic coast, is the centre of Brazilian African culture, with street stalls selling distinctive dishes, such as Moqueca Baiana (fish stew in coconut milk), Acarajé (black-eyed bean fritters) and Vatapá (seafood and nut purée).

Above: The climate of Brazil varies from the mostly tropical north to the temperate zones of the south.

Left: Brazil nuts grow on scattered trees in large forests on the banks of the Amazon, Rio Negro and Orinoco Rivers. The tall trees are climbed with ropes when harvesting.

Above: A vaqueiro herding cattle in the Pantanal wetlands of the southern states of Brazil.

Below right: Clay cooking pots hold the traditional beef stew, barreado, a slow-cooked dish from southern Brazil.

Below: Sunrise on a sugar cane plantation in Sertãozinho, 400km/249 miles from São Paulo.

Fertile farming country

Minas Gerais, in the south-eastern region of Brazil, is noted for its hilly terrain and lush vegetation. In the 17th century it was the epicentre of Brazil's gold rush, and many of the gold miners bred their own pigs to eat. Once the gold rush ended, people turned to farming, and the state became one of the most productive agricultural areas of Brazil. It also attracted many Italian and German immigrants, who were experienced in curing pork to make sausage and ham. The area is still renowned for its mouth-watering pork dishes, such as Porco à Mineira (pork chop served with rice, black beans and greens).

The land around São Paulo is fertile, and the state is a big producer of sugar cane and coffee. The plantations attracted millions of Italian and Asian workers at the beginning of the 20th century, and its inhabitants now consume huge amounts of pizza and pasta.

The traditional central region

The centre of Brazil is an area of amazing bio-diversity, containing savannahs, swamplands and Amazonian forests. The people here eat large quantities of freshwater fish and even some swamp animals, including alligators, armadillos and tapir. Corn is used in many recipes for baked goods and desserts. One special condiment used for flavouring that is rarely found elsewhere is the pequi, an aromatic fruit native to the state of Goiás.

Southern fresh air

German immigrants were attracted by the lower temperatures in the south of Brazil, and settled in the states of Paraná, Santa Catarina and Rio Grande do Sul. This area is the focus of most of Brazil's wine production and is also famous for its large cattle farms, set in the wide grassy plains of the Brazilian Pampas. The local farmers are known as vaqueiros, and their top-quality beef is famous the world over. The most famous culinary tradition of the south is barreado, a beef stew made in a clay pot and cooked in the oven for 12 hours.

Brazilian Eating Traditions

Brazilians have a deep-seated attachment to nature and constantly celebrate their connection with their country through their literature, music, dance and cuisine. The final lines of Brazil's national anthem describe people's relationship with their land in a beautifully poignant way: 'To the sons of this soil you are a gentle mother, beloved nation Brazil'. This relationship is expressed throughout the eating day, especially at mealtimes, which are seen as important family times.

Brazilian meals

Whether at home or in a restaurant, meals are seen as not just a time to eat, but also for spending time with family and friends. Breakfast may be a simple meal of bread and butter with coffee and fresh fruit, but lunch is usually a proper sit-down meal, which can last more than an hour, even on a weekday. The evening meal is, therefore, served much later, or is a much lighter meal.

Cafes and juice bars

Lanche is the Brazilian word for a snack, and when not in the mood for a proper meal Brazilians go to a 'lanchonete' for a quick sandwich or a treat. Behind the glass counter, sweets like Brigadeiros, or savoury bites like empanadas or Kibe, line up waiting for the less calorie-conscious customers.

A recent innovation is buffet restaurants called A Kilo (per kilo) where plates are piled high from the huge variety of dishes available, then charged by weight by the cashier.

In all meals, and as a snack throughout the day, fruit plays a large part in the Brazilian diet, and there are hundreds of juice bars found throughout the cities. These are usually modest establishments whose owners invest more in blenders and sandwich presses than in fancy furniture; customers simply stand by the counter to finish what they have bought.

Some drinks that include milk, cereals and other additives (such as wheatgrass) are referred to as 'vitaminas', a Brazilian version of the smoothie. However, most are made from deliciously ripe fresh fruit, chilled by blending them with crushed ice. One exception is Açaí na Tigeja (açaí in a bowl), which is beaten with sugary guaraná syrup to an ice cream-like consistency and topped with granola and tapioca flakes – a meal in a dish.

Centuries of economic reliance on the cultivation of sugar cane has left most Brazilians positively addicted to sugar. The Portuguese learned very early on how to preserve fruits by boiling them with sugar, and they concocted many desserts such as cocada (shredded coconut and sugar). Many juice bars and lanchonetes sell garapa (freshly pressed sugar cane juice). The stems of sugar cane are pushed through presses into a jar containing a large block of ice, then poured out. Garapa is often served with a Pastel – a fried pastry – a combination which is probably the nation's favourite snack.

Sugar cane is also the base ingredient of Brazil's spirit of choice, cachaça. This is either consumed neat or mixed with fruits, as in the famous lime cocktail Caipirinha.

Left: Pulp of açai, rich in vitamins and antioxidants.

Below: Caipirinha, Brazil's favourite cocktail, made from cachaça – distilled sugar cane – crushed ice and lots of lime.

Bottom: Brazil's favourite snack, Pastel, a deep-fried, filled pastry served with a glass of garapa, sugar cane juice.

Above: A street market stall in the city of Salvador shows the abundance and variety of fruit available in Brazil.

Above right: A waiter serves churrasco at the table, directly from the skewer.

Below right: A plate of Feijoada, Brazil's national dish, often served with rice, Farofa, greens and sliced oranges.

Below: Fresh coconut, ready to drink, on Ipanema Beach, Rio.

The churrasco culture

One of the favourite eating experiences in Brazil is the churrascaria. These are large restaurants specializing in churrasco – grilled meats – that can feed two to three hundred people per session. There is nothing quite like the atmosphere of a churrascaria at Sunday lunchtime: it is sure to be noisy, crowded and good-humoured. The waiters ferry huge quantities of food to the tables, weaving their way between clusters of children, parents, grandparents and friends with a patient smile.

A home-made churrasco usually involves multiple chunks of premium cuts such as best beef steak, ribs, pork loin, coarse pork sausages, chicken breast or even cured cheese, impaled on large skewers and seasoned with nothing more than rock salt, then cooked over a charcoal grill.

Guests bring a dizzying collection of side dishes to accompany the meat, such as Farofas (cassava flour toasted in butter), rice, beans, salads, deep-fried bananas, Molho à Campanha (tomato and onion salsa), corn, potato salad and many others. This sumptuous array of dishes is washed down with large quantities of Caipirinha (cachaça and lime cocktail), batidas (cachaça with fruit juice), beer and wine.

Brazil's favourite party dish

A Feijoada, or pork and bean stew, requires a lot of advance preparation. The meat – beef jerky, sausages, smoked pork ribs, belly, snout, trotters, ears and tails – is soaked overnight, then simmered in large pans for several hours with dried black beans. An hour or so before serving, the Feijoada is seasoned with fried onions and garlic. Side dishes of white rice and sliced oranges accompany the meat.

Malagueta peppers often add the finishing touch to a Feijoada. These small, heavily perfumed hot chillies are usually served in a small pot, mixed with vegetable oil. A few drops are enough to add a shot of heat.

Festivals and celebrations

Brazil has a rich folklore. Throughout its massive territory, thousands of communities celebrate their inherited culture in different ways. There are hundreds of colourful festivals, carnivals, processions, pilgrimages, offering ceremonies and even group blessings, most of which involve delicious food and drink as part of the celebration.

Semana Santa

Holy Week (Semana Santa) is a Catholic celebration that starts on the Sunday before Easter Sunday. Together with Christmas, this is one of the most important events in the church calendar.

Tradition dictates that red meat should be avoided during Holy Week; however, many families apply this rule only to Good Friday. Some cook a large fish or opt for the most traditional of Easter dishes, bacalhau (salt cod), originally a Portuguese favourite. Brazil is one of the world's biggest producers of chocolate, so naturally chocolate eggs are a major part of the celebration.

Festa Junina

The tradition of Festa Junina (June Festivals) celebrates three of the most well-loved Catholic saints in Brazil: Saint John, Saint Peter and Saint Antony. In the north-east it is also a celebration of the arrival of winter and the start of the much-needed rainy season. The corn harvest is under way, so corn features in most of the traditional treats found at June parties: pamonha (corn pudding steamed in corn husks), maize couscous, curau (corn custard), cooked or grilled corn, maize cakes and popcorn.

Indian, African, European and Oriental traditions have also been adopted for these celebrations. Maypole dancing and square dancing comes from Portugal and Spain; the fireworks, firecrackers and flying lanterns

Above: Plates of comida mineira, local food from Minas Gerais, that will fuel hungry carnival participants, together with copious quantities of Caipirinhas.

Above left: One of the elaborate floats in a carnival parade.

Below: Traditionally dressed women taking part in the carnival in Salvador da Bahia.

St Antony's bun
On 13 June, St Antony's Day, churches distribute the specially baked 'St Antony's bun', which is then stored with the other bread in the house to ensure a period of plenty. Superstition says that a single woman who eats the bun will soon find herself a husband.

Right: Revellers gather on Copacabana beach in Rio de Janeiro to ring in the new year.

found on the streets were originally Chinese; and from Africa, there are sweet treats such as Mugunzá (hominy corn porridge), cocada (coconut and sugar bar) and Pé de Moleque (peanut brittle). Quentão, Brazil's answer to mulled wine, adds a Germanic touch.

Christmas

As it comes right in the middle of Brazil's summer it makes sense to celebrate Christmas in the evening. The main meal is therefore held on the night of Christmas Eve.

Despite the high temperatures, roast turkey is the most popular festive meal for Brazilian families, prepared with a stuffing of Farofa (cassava flour toasted with butter) mixed with dried fruit and chestnuts, and accompanied by white rice and gravy. Sweet glazed ham is another favourite and can be served hot or cold. One peculiar tradition is the habit of decorating the turkey with fios d'ovos (egg strings), a Portuguese delicacy made by dribbling egg yolk on boiling sugar syrup. For dessert, many Brazilians will tuck into rabanada, a distant cousin of French toast, made with thick slices of bread covered with a generous layer of sugar and cinnamon.

Below: A girl in Minas Gerais, dressed as an angel, holds a chalice during Semana Santa or Holy Week celebrations, which end on Easter day.

New Year's Eve

Brazilians use the French word 'Reveillon' instead of New Year's Eve, and it is celebrated with great enthusiasm, both in lavish house parties and in public gatherings followed by impressive firework displays.

In Rio de Janeiro, Brazil's African inheritance takes centre stage on the last day of the year. Thousands of devout followers of the Candomblé religion flock to the sands of Copacabana beach to celebrate Yemanjá, the African deity known as the 'Queen of the Sea'. Hundreds of little boats carrying flowers, perfume, candles and other offerings are launched, covering the calm waters of Copacabana with twinkling lights.

Reveillon dinner is usually a very luxurious meal, with preference given to dishes that can be served cold during this hot season, such as cold meats, terrines, savoury mousses, pies, salads and plenty of fruit. There are numerous superstitions associated with the day, such as not eating poultry (as they walk backwards while pecking for food), or chewing seven pomegranate seeds and keeping their husks in a piece of paper concealed in your wallet to attract good fortune in the coming year.

Brazil's Favourite Ingredients

Brazil is a rich and productive country, and the sheer variety of fruits, vegetables, fish and meat eaten within its borders is amazing. Certain Brazilian favourites, such as brazil nuts, are now exported all around the world, whereas other typical ingredients like cassava, guava and palm hearts are more restricted to local cooks. However, they can be found all around the world in small Portuguese groceries, through online suppliers, and in health food shops.

Meat, poultry and game

Two kinds of meat reign supreme in Brazil: beef and pork. The best beef is served quite simply as a juicy steak, while lesser cuts are stewed gently with vegetables or turned into one of the quintessential Brazilian ingredients, carne seca (Brazilian beef jerky or dried beef). This product was created due to the necessity of keeping meat fresh in the hot, dry climate of the north-east. It features as the main ingredient in Jabá com Jerimum (beef jerky and pumpkin) or in a minor role in a Feijoada (black bean stew). The favourite cut of beef for a barbecue is picanha, which is taken from the very top of the rump. It is covered by a thick layer of fat, which keeps the meat moist and gives it a strong, almost gamey taste.

There are two types of pork sausage in Brazil: salsicha (processed meat sausages resembling frankfurters) and linguiça (a sausage with visible large meat chunks). Salsichas are usually used for hot dogs, and linguiças are delicious when fried, cut and served like cocktail sausages. Thicker versions (often called calabresa) feature in barbecues or one of the meats in a feijoada.

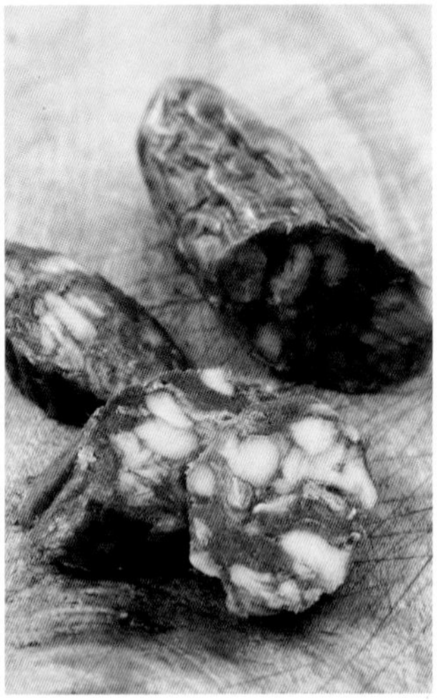

Fish and shellfish

Many of the sea and river fish eaten in Brazil are known only in that country. Luckily, the kinds of white fish available everywhere can be substituted for the local Brazilian fish with a similar result – for example, try a mixture of cod, haddock, plaice or turbot in a mixed fish stew or fish soup. The sauces surrounding the fish are all-important, the individual flavour of each fish less so. The focus is more on the other delicious treats to be found in the seas

Above: The Brazilian version of chorizo, chouriço, is often used as a flavouring in soups and stews.

Above left: Picanha, a cut of beef also known as top rump.

Below, from left to right: tilapia fillets, grouper, red mullet and dried shrimp.

Below, from top to bottom: Black-eyed beans (peas), black beans, hominy, and palm hearts.

and rivers, such as octopus, prawns (shrimp) and crab. Brazil produces a huge quantity of prawns in its seaside fish farms. Some of the smaller shrimp are salted and dried in the sun, and these intense, tasty morsels, known as camarão seco, are used to add a depth and pungent flavour to recipes such as Xinxim de Galinha (chicken and prawn stew) or Vatapá (seafood and nut purée).

Vegetables

Nearly all Brazilians eat beans on a daily basis. Black beans appear as the main ingredient of Brazil's national dish, Feijoada, while in the north and west of the country, preference shifts to other types of bean, such as mulatinho (small red kidney beans), feijão de corda, fradinho (black-eyed beans (peas)), carioca, roxinho and many others.

Corn is the most popular grain in Brazil. As a fresh product it is used in recipes such as curau (corn custard) and pamonha (steamed creamed corn). It is also milled into flour (fubá), which is used in Bolo de Fubá (maize cake) and polenta (corn flour mash), a popular side dish served with stews.

Cassava, or manioc, is a root vegetable that grows abundantly throughout Brazil and was used by the Brazilian Indians for thousands of years. Their method for processing cassava (which is poisonous raw) created by-products such as a grainy flour (farinha de mandioca) and a pure starch (polvilho), which have become very popular with all Brazilians. The root itself and both types of flour it produces are consumed in huge amounts. The root is often boiled as a replacement for potatoes, mashed in dishes such as Escondidinho de Carne Seca (beef jerky and cassava purée cottage pie) and Bobó de Camarão (prawns in cassava sauce), or deep fried as chips (fries).

Cassava flour is used to thicken sauces, or add crunch to stews or beans. It is also served simply toasted with butter, and mixed with a variety of ingredients to make Farofa. The pure starch, polvinho, is available in doce

Above: The two types of cassava flour, used in numerous ways in Brazilian cooking; untoasted (top) and toasted (bottom).

(sweet) or azedo (sour) varieties and is used to make Tapioca Beiju (tapioca pancakes) and Pão de Queijo (cheesy dough balls).

Palm hearts are extracted from the growing bud of palm trees. They are preserved in brine and sold in cans or jars. The fibrous but creamy texture makes them popular in salads or just on their own with a drizzle of olive oil, but they are also used in several recipes such as Pastelão de Frango e Palmito (chicken and palm hearts pie) or even as a pizza topping.

Nuts and fruit

The exotic fruits found growing in Brazil are beginning to be better known in other parts of the world, but some are still best appreciated in their country of origin – for example, caju, a delicious fruit with a soft, sweet pulp that is often made into juices or cocktails. Outside Brazil, people tend to eat only the caju nut (cashew). Peanuts are planted in vast quantities throughout Brazil and peanut oil is popular in cooking. The nuts are used in peanut brittle or sold freshly roasted by

Dendê Oil

Palm oil, known in Brazil as dendê oil, is a thick, reddish-orange, strong-flavoured oil extracted from the pulp of a fruit from a type of palm tree grown in Africa and in Brazil. It has a very distinctive smell and taste, and is used in cooking throughout Brazil, particularly in Baian dishes.

street vendors, who will often place a handful on bar tables as a sample. Brazil nuts, called castanhas do pará, are the largest export from the Amazon. They are very popular in the north of the country, where they are often used for baking.

Guavas are native fruits of Central and South America. There are two kinds available: white-fleshed and red-fleshed. The white guava is most commonly eaten in its natural form, and the red one is the main ingredient of goiabada, a thick guava preserve available in many textures, from soft and spreadable to a solid block sometimes called guava cheese. Another of Brazil's quintessential flavours, maracujá (passion fruit) is the tough-skinned fruit of the maracujá vine. It is aromatic, with tart, sweet juice and tiny pips. It can be eaten fresh, split open and sprinkled with sugar, but most of the crop is destined for the juice and essence market. The xuxu pear, or chayote, is the fruit of a wild creeper that grows pretty much anywhere in Brazil. Its pulp has a bland taste similar to a watered down courgette (zucchini). Xuxu must be cooked before being eaten but can be served hot (sautéed with butter and parsley) or cold in salads.

Açaí is the berry of the açaí palm, native to the tropical north and north-east of Brazil. The deep blue-purple pulp is separated from the pip, then mashed and frozen for storage.

Avocados are very plentiful in Brazil and trees can often be found in squares and other public places. They are larger than the Hess variety and sold ripe in most stores. Their flesh is very light and sweet, which explains why most Brazilians see it as dessert.

The humble lime is a must-have in every Brazilian house. It is used as a marinade for fish or pork, as well as for making juices, cocktails, sorbets, desserts and cakes. The most-used ingredient after cassava must be the coconut, its flesh featuring in numerous sweet and savoury Brazilian dishes, and its water used for a refreshing health drink.

Dairy

There are many varieties of cheese in Brazil, usually pale in colour and sold while still fresh rather than matured. For example, queijo minas is a fresh curd cheese, sold within days of manufacture in sealed pots that retain the whey. It is used in sandwiches, salads and desserts. Queijo coalho is a firm, lightweight cheese, quite salty in taste and squeaky in texture, similar to Greek halloumi. It is often found on street stalls, freshly grilled.

Catupiry is the brand name of Brazil's most famous requeijão, a processed cheese halfway between cheese and cream. It appears everywhere, from the filling for the country's favourite snack, Pastel (filled pastry) to the sauce for guava soufflé. Catupiry is rarely available outside Brazil, but a soft curd or cream cheese is an acceptable substitute.

Leite Moça (condensed milk) is incredibly popular in Brazil. It was first imported from

Top: Xuxu pear.
Above: Tapioca.

Below: Monkey nuts.
Bottom: Cassava.

Above: Coconut is added to hundreds of Brazilian recipes, both savoury and sweet.

Above right: Brigadeiro truffles are made out of the much-loved condensed milk, known by its brand name of Leite Moça.

Below, top to bottom: Açaí pulp, and chillies.

Bottom right: Hot pepper sauce.

Above: Coffee is drunk throughout the day, often black and very sweet.

Switzerland in 1890, and the naturally sweet tooth of most Brazilians, combined with the practicality of this way of preserving milk, must have helped its adoption. Condensed milk is used in thousands of recipes in Brazil, from a traditional Pudim de Leite (caramel custard) to drinks such as Batida de Côco (coconut and cachaça cocktail).

Red pepper sauce

Known in Portugal and Mozambique as piri piri, the malagueta pepper is a small green pepper that turns red as it ripens, and packs quite a punch. It is often brought to the table in small pots, infused in oil, to be added to the plate by each diner. There are many brands that produce similar red peppery sauces.

Drinks

Both alcoholic concoctions and non-alcoholic soft drinks are consumed in quantities in this hot country. The juice bars lining the streets in major cities and towns are marvellous sources of all kinds of fruit drinks based on the produce of the countryside. When it comes to something more alcoholic, the most popular spirit sold in Brazil is cachaça, a liquor distilled from sugar cane. It is the main ingredient of Brazil's favourite cocktail, Caipirinha, made with cachaça, sugar and lime.

In the south, the favourite hot drink is mate, consumed from calabash gourds and sipped through a metal spoon or straw with strainer holes at the bottom. Iced mate is a hugely popular drink, served by vendors who carry drums of it up and down the beaches.

Brazil is the world's biggest producer and exporter of coffee, with an enormous harvest from its colonial plantations. It is drunk several times a day in tiny cups with plenty of sugar. The ritual of coffee drinking is a welcome break in the working day, and many meetings are transferred to the nearest bar.

Coloral

Brazilian recipes requiring a boost of red earthiness generally use coloral rather than paprika. Coloral is a potent red powder made from grinding the dry seeds of the urucum, an Amazonian fruit used by the Brazilian Indians to paint their faces and bodies during rituals and celebrations.

Street Food and Snacks

Brazilians are active people, always on the go. Most of them rely on quick, filling snacks to keep energy levels up during the hustle and bustle of their working day, and for an often hectic nightlife.

Quick snacks for people on the move

Filling snacks such as a Pastel (a pocket of deep-fried flaky pastry with a savoury filling, usually soft cheese) or Kibe (deep-fried Lebanese meat balls) are good substitutes for lunch, and are easy enough to eat while standing at one of the numerous stalls in the street markets, or sunning yourself on the beach. Surfers are particularly keen on a dish of sweet Cuscuz de Tapioca com Coco, a semi-solid block of tapioca pudding covered in grated coconut and drizzled with condensed milk. Another sustaining favourite is a bowl of Açaí na tigeja, made with the delicious, strong-tasting berry from the açaí palm, bought ready-made from one of the thousands of juice bars found in every town.

Night-time socializing in Brazil requires pace and stamina. Through a long evening of drinking, chatting and dancing, which often requires moving from bar to bar in search of different groups of friends, snacks are available to line the stomach while keeping people's options open for a larger meal later. Golden chunks of Aipim Frito (cassava chips), a portion of Bolinho de Bacalhau (salt cod fritters) or a steaming shot of Caldinho de Feijão (black bean soup) keep the revellers happy and full of energy, ready to show off their moves on the dance floor.

Right middle: A roof top view of the baroque buildings of the district of Pelourinho, in the city of Salvador, Bahia.
Page 21: Spices and flavourings on sale in a street market.

Salt cod fritters

Bolinho de bacalhau

Brazilians love their salgadinhos (appetizers), which are eaten as snacks throughout the day. Portuguese in origin, these delicious salt cod fritters can be found wherever ice-cold beer is served. You will need to begin this dish a day or two in advance to allow time to soak the fish.

Makes about 25

- 450g/1lb salt cod
- 400g/14oz/2 cups cold mashed potatoes
- 15ml/1 tbsp finely chopped fresh parsley
- 3 eggs, separated
- 15ml/1 tbsp olive oil
- 115g/4oz/1 cup dry breadcrumbs
- ground black pepper
- vegetable oil for deep-frying
- lime wedges and hot pepper sauce, to serve

1 Put the salt cod in a large bowl and cover with plenty of cold water. Leave to soak in the refrigerator for 24–36 hours, changing the water at least three times to remove the salt.

2 Drain the cod and place in a pan with fresh cold water. Bring to the boil, lower the heat and simmer for 15 minutes. Drain and set the fish aside to cool. When the fish is cold, discard any skin and bones, place in a food processor and pulse a few times to shred; do not purée.

3 Put the shredded fish, mashed potatoes, chopped parsley, egg yolks and olive oil in a bowl. Season with pepper and mix well.

4 In a separate bowl, whisk the egg whites until stiff peaks form, then carefully fold them into the fish and potato mixture.

5 Put the breadcrumbs in a wide shallow bowl or on a plate.

6 Using a tablespoon, scoop up the mixture into walnut-sized balls and roll between the palms of your hands.

7 Roll a few balls at a time in the breadcrumbs to coat, then transfer to a baking tray. Chill in the refrigerator for 30 minutes to firm them up.

8 Heat a 7.5cm/3in depth of vegetable oil in a deep, heavy pan to 180°C/350°F on a sugar thermometer. Fry the salt cod fritters in small batches until golden. Drain on kitchen paper, transfer to a baking tray, and keep warm in a low oven while cooking the rest.

9 Serve hot, garnished with wedges of lime, and accompanied by hot pepper sauce.

Cook's tip These fritters can be made in advance and fried straight from frozen at a slightly lower temperature of 170°C/340°F.

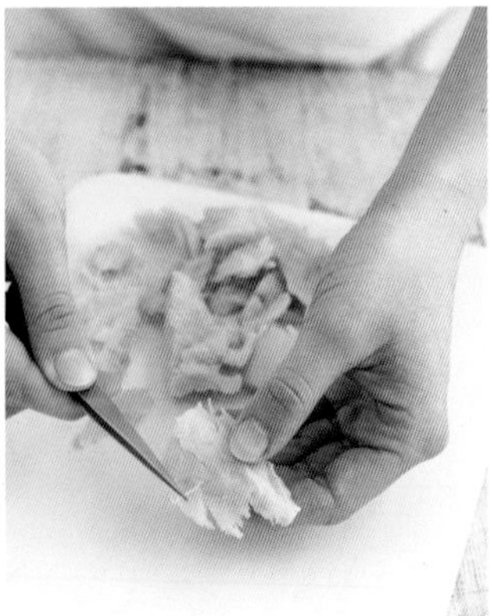

Energy 100kcal/414kJ; Protein 6.5g; Carbohydrate 3.5, of which sugars 0.1g; Fat 6.5g, of which saturates 0.9g; Cholesterol 28mg; Calcium 47mg; Fibre 0.3g; Sodium 804mg

Lebanese meat fritters

Kibe

Kibe (or Quibe), pronounced 'kee-bee' is the Brazilian version of the Lebanese kibbeh – an oval-shaped croquette made with minced meat and bulgur wheat. The original recipe was brought to Brazil by Lebanese immigrants in the early 1900s, and although it continues to be referred to as 'Arab Food', it is now thought of as a national classic, and is sold in restaurants and bars all over the country.

Makes 12

For the kibe:

250g/9oz/1¼ cups bulgur wheat

1kg/2¼ lb extra-lean minced (ground) lamb

1 large onion, finely chopped

115g/4oz/2 cups fresh mint, chopped

2.5-5ml/½–1 tsp ground white pepper

5ml/1 tsp freshly grated nutmeg

5ml/1 tsp ground cinnamon

5ml/1 tsp salt

vegetable oil, for deep frying

For the filling:

30ml/2 tbsp vegetable oil

½ onion, finely chopped

400g/14oz extra-lean minced (ground) beef

50g/2oz/½ cup pine nuts

30ml/2 tbsp parsley, chopped

30ml/2 tbsp spring onions (scallions), finely chopped

wedges of lime, hummus and hot pepper sauce, to serve

Cook's tip If you don't have a meat grinder, you can grind the meat by hand using a large mortar and pestle.

1 Soak the bulgur wheat in a large bowl, according to the instructions on the packet. Drain well and tip back into the bowl.

2 Add the minced lamb, onion, mint, pepper, nutmeg, cinnamon and salt to the bulgur, and mix thoroughly.

3 Put the mixture through a meat grinder to produce a finely chopped paste; don't try to use a food processor as the meat will turn into a purée, while the bulgur wheat remains whole. Chill in the refrigerator until ready to use.

4 To make the filling, heat the oil in a pan and cook the onion for 5 minutes, until beginning to soften. Add the minced beef and fry until it is brown and all the liquid has evaporated. Add the pine nuts, parsley and spring onions, and stir-fry for another minute. Set aside to cool.

5 Remove the lamb and bulgur wheat mixture from the refrigerator. To make each kibe, scoop up a piece of paste and shape into a round slightly bigger than a golf ball.

6 Press your thumb into the ball and gently squeeze the paste around it with your other hand to make a cup-like shape. Fill the hole with a teaspoon of the beef filling.

7 Pat the filling down gently and then close the hole by pinching the edges together. Use a gently squeezing and rolling motion with the palms of your hands to taper two sides, making it into a torpedo shape.

8 Heat a 10cm/4in depth of vegetable oil in a deep, heavy pan to 170°C/340°F on a sugar thermometer. Fry the kibes in batches of three or four until dark golden. Drain on kitchen paper and keep warm on a baking tray in a low oven while cooking the remainder.

9 Garnish with wedges of lime and serve with some hummus and hot pepper sauce.

Cook's tip Check that the kibe are cooked through by cutting one open; the meat in the middle should be brown, not pink, and the centre is piping hot.

Energy 397kcal/1652kJ; Protein 26.2g; Carbohydrate 18.6g, of which sugars 1.8g; Fat 24.4g, of which saturates 7.3g; Cholesterol 84mg; Calcium 39mg; Fibre 0.5 g; Sodium 239mg

Beef jerky and cassava purée cottage pie

Escondidinho de carne seca

Cured dried beef, or jerky, is widely consumed throughout Brazil and, at its best, is as prized an ingredient as a good Serrano ham would be in Spain. Escondidinho means 'well hidden', alluding to the fact that the delicious filling lies hidden beneath a plain-looking topping. The pie can be served as a main dish, but in many bars it is served as a snack in tiny single portions.

1 Peel the cassava root and cut into large chunks. Cook in lightly salted boiling water for about 20 minutes, until tender.

2 Drain the cassava and, when cool enough to handle, remove and discard any tough thick fibres in the centre of the root, then mash the cassava thoroughly with the butter and cream. Season with salt (remember that the beef jerky will be fairly salty) and pepper.

3 Heat the oil in a large frying pan and add the sliced onion. Fry for 8–10 minutes, until it starts to brown.

4 Add the shredded beef jerky and the garlic to the onion and fry for a couple of minutes, then add the diced tomato and parsley and fry for another 3–4 minutes. Preheat the oven to 190°C/375°F/Gas 5.

5 To assemble each pie, place a layer of the shredded beef jerky on the bottom of a large ramekin or small ovenproof dish.

6 Cover the meat with a layer of cassava mash, smoothing it to the sides.

7 Top the layer of cassava mash with little lumps of cream cheese, and finally a sprinkling of grated Cheddar or Gouda cheese.

8 Bake in the oven for 10-15 minutes until the cheese melts and starts to bubble. Serve immediately.

Cook's tip You can buy beef jerky already tenderized and shredded. If you want to prepare your own, buy at least 450g/1lb to allow for wastage, as the quality of jerky varies.

Cut into chunks and boil for 45 minutes to 1 hour, replacing the water with fresh boiling water from the kettle at least three times to remove the salt. Taste the beef jerky after boiling to ensure enough of the salt has been removed, and boil once more in fresh water if necessary. Let it cool completely, then shred it by pulling the fibres apart with your fingers. Remove and discard any pieces of sinew.

Serves 6

500g/1¼lb cassava root

15ml/1 tbsp butter

200ml/7fl oz/scant 1 cup double (heavy) cream

30ml/2 tbsp vegetable oil

½ medium onion, thinly sliced

350g/12oz cleaned, shredded beef jerky

2 garlic cloves, crushed

1 large tomato, peeled, seeded and diced

15g/½ oz/¼ cup finely chopped fresh parsley

225g/8oz/1 cup cream cheese

115g/4oz/1 cup Cheddar or Gouda cheese, grated

salt and ground black pepper

Energy 841kcal/3499kJ; Protein 26.9g; Carbohydrate 39.7g, of which sugars 8.6g; Fat 64.6g, of which saturates 34.8g; Cholesterol 133mg; Calcium 230mg; Fibre 3.1g; Sodium 1560mg

Pastel pastries with meat filling

Pastel de feira de carne

The secret of this crisp and flaky pastry is the addition of a little cachaça. One of the most popular savoury 'pastels' sold on the streets is packed with a mixture of well-browned lean minced beef, simply flavoured with garlic, onions, parsley and a generous amount of salty green olives.

Makes about 6

For the pastel pastry

- 260g/9½oz/scant 2¾ cups plain (all-purpose) flour
- 5ml/1 tsp salt
- 30ml/2 tbsp lard or white cooking fat, diced
- 5ml/1 tsp cachaça or vodka
- 15ml/1 tbsp white vinegar
- 120ml/4fl oz/½ cup warm water

For the meat filling

- ¼ onion, finely chopped
- 400g/14oz lean minced (ground) beef
- 2 cloves garlic, crushed
- 40g/1½oz/¼ cup green olives, sliced
- 15ml/1 tbsp parsley, chopped
- 15ml/1 tbsp finely chopped spring onions (scallions)
- ground black pepper
- hot pepper sauce, ketchup, Worcestershire sauce or mustard, to serve

1 To make the pastry, sift the flour and salt into a large bowl. Rub in the lard with your fingertips until the mixture resembles fine breadcrumbs.

2 Stir in the cachaça and white vinegar, then gradually mix in the warm water; you may not need it all, so add a little at a time until the mixture forms a rough, dry dough.

3 Transfer to a lightly floured surface and knead for 3–4 minutes until you have a smooth but fairly stiff dough. Shape into a roll with a diameter of about 5cm/2in. Wrap in clear film (plastic wrap) and leave at room temperature for at least 4 hours.

4 Cut the dough into six pieces. Using a rolling pin or pasta machine, roll each piece until a little thinner than 3mm/⅛in, then trim into a 10 x 20cm/4 x 8in rectangle. Use straight away, or make a stack of rectangles, adding baking parchment between each layer.

5 Tightly cover the whole stack with clear film and refrigerate until needed. You can store the dough for up to four days before using.

6 To make the beef filling, heat 30ml/2 tbsp vegetable oil in a frying pan and fry the onion until almost soft. Add the beef and garlic, and cook until the meat is brown and the liquid has evaporated. Stir the olives, parsley and spring onions into the pan, and season with pepper to taste. Remove from the heat and leave to cool.

7 Place six pastry rectangles on a floured surface and brush the edges with water. Add a tablespoon of cold filling to one half of the rectangle and fold the other half over it. Press the edges together firmly, then use a fork to mark a pattern round the edges of each pastel.

8 Heat a 7.5cm/3in depth of vegetable oil in a deep pan to 190°C/375°F on a sugar thermometer. Fry the pastries, one at a time until golden and crisp. Use slotted spoons to turn them over every 30 seconds, so that they brown on both sides.

9 When golden, remove from the pan, drain on kitchen paper, and keep warm. Serve hot with hot pepper sauce, ketchup, Worcestershire sauce, or mustard.

Energy 342kcal/1433kJ; Protein 18.9g; Carbohydrate 34.5g, of which sugars 1.2g; Fat 15.1g, of which saturates 4.4g; Cholesterol 47mg; Calcium 75mg; Fibre 2.1g; Sodium 286mg

Deep-fried pastry with cheese filling.

Pastel de feira de queijo

Mozzarella cheese is another classic pastel filling, its soft stretchy texture contrasting beautifully with the deep-fried crisp pastry dough. You could also try a pizza-like version with cheese, chopped tomatoes and fresh oregano.

1 Place six pastry rectangles on a floured surface and lightly brush the edges with water.

2 Put a heaped tablespoonful of grated cheese in the centre of one half of each rectangle, and fold the other half over it. If using a harder cheese, cut a slice about 4cm/1½in square and no thicker than 1cm/½in.

3 Firmly press the edges together, then, using a fork, mark a pattern all around the edges.

4 Heat a 7.5cm/3in depth of vegetable oil in a deep pan to 190°C/375°F on a sugar thermometer. Fry the pastries, one at a time until golden and crisp. Use metal slotted spoons to turn them over every 30 seconds, so that they brown on both sides.

5 Drain on kitchen paper and keep warm in a low oven while cooking the remainder. Serve hot with Worcestershire sauce, hot pepper sauce, ketchup or chutney.

Makes 6

1 quantity of pastel pastry (see page 31)

For the filling

200g/7oz/2 cups grated (shredded) mozzarella

Brazilian-style Salsa (see page 96), Worcestershire sauce, hot pepper sauce, ketchup or chutney, to serve

Cook's tip The insides are very hot, so let the pastries cool a little before serving.

Energy 278kcal/1167kJ; Protein 10.3g; Carbohydrate 33.7g, of which sugars 0.7g; Fat 12.3g, of which saturates 6.7g; Cholesterol 24mg; Calcium 181mg; Fibre 1.6g; Sodium 461mg

Tapioca pancakes

Beiju (or Tapioca)

Serves 6

450g/1lb/4 cups sour cassava starch

285ml/9fl oz/1 cup plus 2 tbsp water

butter and salt, to serve

Variation For a sweet version, instead of sprinkling with salt and spreading with butter, drizzle with condensed milk and scatter with fresh coconut shavings.

For centuries, native Brazilians have made flour from cassava root. It comes in three types: plain, sweet and sour. The latter is used to make a thin, chewy pancake, called beiju in the north of the country, and tapioca in the south.

1 Put the cassava starch in a bowl and drizzle half the water over it. Use your hands to mix, breaking up any large clumps. Gradually add the rest of the water, mixing in the same way.

2 Push the mixture, a little at a time, through a sieve (strainer). The resulting mixture should look like grated Parmesan cheese.

3 Heat a small heavy non-stick frying pan over a low heat.

4 Sprinkle a thin, even layer of the cassava over the base of the pan, leaving no gaps or holes.

5 Cook for 1 minute, then lift the edges of the pancake with a spatula and shake the pan to loosen it from the bottom. Turn over or flip the pancake and cook the other side for 1 minute.

6 Slide the pancake on to a plate, spread generously with butter, and sprinkle with salt. Roll up and serve straight away.

Energy 266kcal/1131kJ; Protein 0.5g; Carbohydrate 69g, of which sugars 0g; Fat 0.5g, of which saturates 0.1g; Cholesterol 0mg; Calcium 11mg; Fibre 0.0 g; Sodium 105mg

Black-eyed bean fritters with prawn sauce

Acarajé

Acarajé are bean fritters originally made and sold on the streets of the city of Salvador by the 'Baianas' – female vendors dressed in frilly white cotton dresses and traditional African headscarves – as the recipe was taken to Brazil by the slaves from the West African coast. They are usually deep-fried in palm oil (dendê) which gives them their reddish colour, then split in half and filled with all kinds of different sauces, making them a challenge to eat without making a mess.

Makes about 20

300g/11oz/scant 2 cups black-eyed beans (peas), soaked overnight in cold water

¼ medium onion, roughly chopped

salt and black pepper

a mixture (half and half) of palm oil (dendê) and vegetable oil, to deep-fry

For the sauce:

30ml/2 tbsp olive oil

½ onion, finely chopped

2 cloves garlic, crushed

150g/5oz dried shrimp

2 green chillies (optional), seeded and finely chopped

400g/14oz can chopped plum tomatoes

200g/7oz small cooked prawns (shrimp), peeled

25g/1oz/½ cup fresh coriander (cilantro), finely chopped

salt and ground black pepper

lime wedges and hot pepper sauce, to serve

1 Drain the soaked beans and place in a food processor. Pulse a couple of times to break up the beans. Tip them back into the bowl and cover with water. Using your hands, gently squeeze and stir the beans to release the skins. Let the skins float to the top, scoop them out with your hands and repeat until all the skins are gone. Drain well. Mix in the chopped onion.

2 Working in batches, process the beans and onion until you achieve a smooth paste, similar in consistency to hummus. Add salt and pepper to taste, stir and set aside.

3 For the sauce, heat the olive oil in a pan and gently fry the onion for 10 minutes until soft. Add the garlic, dried shrimp, and chopped chillies (if using). Fry for a further 2–3 minutes.

4 Add the tomatoes, cooked prawns and chopped coriander, and season to taste with salt and black pepper. Simmer for 4–6 minutes, then leave to cool.

5 Heat a 7.5cm/3in depth of palm oil and vegetable oil in a deep pan to 190°C/375°F on a sugar thermometer. Using two spoons, scoop up some of the purée and make a large quenelle, then gently slide it into the oil. Fry for 7–8 minutes, turning to brown both sides. Drain on kitchen paper and keep warm.

6 Serve the fritters hot with a bowl of the prawn sauce, wedges of lime to squeeze over and hot pepper sauce.

Cook's tip Check the fritters are cooked through by cutting one in half. They should have a dry, firm, bread-like consistency inside.

Energy 137kcal/572kJ; Protein 10.1g; Carbohydrate 8.8g, of which sugars 0.9g; Fat 7g, of which saturates 1.8g; Cholesterol 66mg; Calcium 116mg; Fibre 0.1; Sodium 526mg

Black bean pick-me-up

Caldinho de feijão

Serves 6

15ml/1 tbsp vegetable oil

225g/8oz bacon lardons, or pork scratchings

450g/1lb Everyday Black Beans (see page 87)

250ml/8fl oz/1 cup water

salt and ground black pepper

olive oil, to drizzle

30ml/2 tbsp fresh parsley, chopped

Although it sounds unusual, little shots of soup are often served at Brazilian bars to accompany your drink, and they go surprisingly well with cold beer and cocktails. This tasty version is made more substantial with the addition of crispy bacon.

1 Heat the vegetable oil in a deep frying pan and fry the bacon lardons until crispy. Transfer to a plate lined with kitchen paper to drain, and allow to cool.

2 Put the black beans and water in a food processor or blender and season with salt and pepper. Blend to a smooth purée.

3 Pour into a small pan, bring to the boil and simmer for 5 minutes.

4 Pour or ladle the soup into small heatproof glasses or porcelain espresso cups. Garnish with a drizzle of olive oil, a generous sprinkling of chopped parsley and bacon lardons or crumbled pork scratchings. Serve piping hot.

Energy 320kcal/1333kJ; Protein 21.3g; Carbohydrate 8.6g, of which sugars 1.8g; Fat 22.5g, of which saturates 0.7g; Cholesterol 0mg; Calcium 48mg; Fibre 14.1g; Sodium 746mg

Green broth

Caldo verde

Originally from Portugal, 'caldo verde' is a light soup that is well suited to the mild winters of Brazil's southern states. The broth, combined with the peppery taste of the spring greens and smoky chouriço sausage, makes this sophisticated comfort food. If you can't find Portuguese chouriço, use Spanish chorizo instead.

1 Heat the oil in a large pan over a medium heat. Add the onions and cook gently for 8–10 minutes, until soft. Add the garlic and half the chouriço and cook for 2 minutes, stirring.

2 Add the potatoes and water, bring to the boil, then lower the heat, half-cover the pan with a lid and simmer for 15 minutes, or until the potatoes are just tender. Remove from the heat and set aside to cool for 5 minutes.

3 Purée the soup in a food processor or blender, in batches, if necessary, then pour back into the pan. Add the spring greens, bring to the boil, cover and simmer for 2–3 minutes, or until tender.

4 Season to taste with salt and pepper and ladle into warmed bowls. Serve piping hot, garnished with the remaining cubes of chouriço and a drizzle of olive oil.

Serves 6

- 60ml/4 tbsp olive oil, plus extra to drizzle
- 1 large onion, chopped
- 2 cloves garlic, finely chopped
- 200g/7oz chouriço, or chorizo, cubed
- 675g/1½ lb potatoes, peeled and diced
- 2 litres/3½ pints/8 cups cold water
- 350g/12oz spring greens (collards), finely shredded
- salt and ground black pepper

Cook's tip When preparing the spring greens, remove the tough stalks, then roll each leaf up tightly and shred as finely as possible with a sharp knife.

Energy 328kcal/1366kJ; Protein 10.7g; Carbohydrate 25.5g, of which sugars 5.4g; Fat 21g, of which saturates 5g; Cholesterol 0mg; Calcium 138mg; Fibre 6 g; Sodium 276mg

Deep-fried chunky cassava chips

Aipim frito

Cassava grows well in hot and humid climates, and features in many Brazilian recipes from main courses to desserts, bread and cakes. Because it has a high starch content, it makes delicious chips that are crunchy on the outside and fluffy in the middle, so an evening out often begins with an order of this popular bar snack.

1 Peel the cassava and cut across its width into three chunks. Peel the onion and spike it with the cloves, then put it in a large pan.

2 Add plenty of water to the pan – you'll need about 3 litres/5¼ pints/12 cups – and add the salt. Add the cassava root and bring to the boil.

3 Turn down the heat, half cover the pan with a lid and simmer for 20 minutes, or until the cassava is tender. Drain and set aside to cool. When cool enough to handle, insert a small knife into the chunks and twist them open.

4 Remove any tough fibres from the middle of the cassava chunks and discard. Cut the cassava into chip-sized wedges.

5 Heat a 7.5cm/3in depth of vegetable oil in a deep pan until it registers 190°C/375°F on a sugar thermometer. Fry in two or three batches for 3 minutes. Drain and set aside to cool.

6 After all the wedges are fried and cooled, reheat the oil and fry again until golden and crispy. Drain and place on a plate lined with kitchen paper. Add salt and serve immediately.

Serves 6

1 large cassava root, about 675g/1½ lb in weight

1 onion

24 whole cloves

30ml/2 tbsp salt

vegetable oil for deep-frying

Cook's tip Test the cassava is tender by piercing with the tip of a knife; it should slide into the middle with ease. Larger parts of the root will start to split, a good indication that it is cooked.

Variation For a tasty alternative, sprinkle some freshly grated Parmesan or Pecorino cheese over the chips and put them in a hot oven for a couple of minutes until the cheese melts.

Energy 295kcal/1237kJ; Protein 0.7g; Carbohydrate 41.4g, of which sugars 1.7g; Fat 15.2g, of which saturates 1.2g; Cholesterol 0mg; Calcium 21mg; Fibre 1.9g; Sodium 1971mg

Coconut and tapioca cake

Cuscuz de tapioca com coco

Serves 8

250g/9oz/1½ cups tapioca (tapioca granules)

2.5ml/½ tsp salt

400ml/14fl oz/1⅔ cups water

120ml/4fl oz/½ cup full-fat (whole) milk

100ml/3½fl oz/scant ½ cup coconut milk

175g/6oz/¾ cup caster (superfine) sugar

200g/7oz freshly grated coconut

extra grated coconut and condensed milk, to serve

This is a sweet and sticky snack made from tapioca, served in slices topped with a fluffy layer of freshly grated coconut and a generous drizzle of condensed milk. Given its high calorie content, low price and easy-to-eat consistency, it is sold in huge quantities at beach locations and is especially popular with surfers.

1 Put the tapioca and salt in a large heatproof bowl. Heat the water, milk, coconut milk and sugar in a pan, stirring occasionally until the sugar has dissolved.

2 When the milk is hot, but not boiling, pour it over the tapioca and stir well. Cover the bowl with a pan lid and leave for 5 minutes, then add half the grated coconut and stir again.

3 Pour the mixture into a lightly greased 20–23cm/8–9in square dish or cake tin (pan).

4 Scatter the remaining grated coconut on top and set aside to cool. When completely cold, chill for at least 2 hours until set and firm.

5 Serve by cutting slices directly from the container, and top with extra grated coconut and a drizzle of condensed milk.

Cook's tip For a softer and moister result, ideal as a dessert rather than a portable snack, add 45ml/3 tbsp more milk or coconut milk to the mixture.

Energy 299kcal/1260kJ; Protein 1.5g; Carbohydrate 54.9g, of which sugars 25.2g; Fat 9.7g, of which saturates 8.2g; Cholesterol 2mg; Calcium 29mg; Fibre 3.1g; Sodium 150mg

Açaí in a bowl

Açaí na tigeja

Açaí berries come from palm trees that are indigenous to the Brazilian rain forest. The small deep purple berries have been used for hundreds of years by tribes for their perceived medicinal properties. In recent years the berry has become a popular health-food supplement not only in Brazil, but internationally. Juices, smoothies and mousse-like sweet soups are sold from beach-front huts and makeshift bars all along Brazil's coast. Açaí has a similar texture to dates, but not the sweetness, which is why people tend to add a lot of sugar or syrup.

1 Put the açaí pulp, syrup or honey, water and ice in a bowl and, using a hand-held blender, blend until smooth. If the mixture is too thick to blend, stop the blender and stir.

2 Slice a banana and pour the açaí mixture into a small bowl. Serve immediately, garnishing the top with a few banana slices along with a sprinkling of granola.

Serves 1

250ml/8fl oz/1cup açai pulp

100ml/3½fl oz/scant ½ cup guaraná syrup or clear honey, or to taste

120ml/4fl oz/½ cup water, preferably chilled

250ml/8fl oz/1 cup crushed ice

banana and granola, to serve

Cook's tip: A favourite in Brazil, guaraná syrup is a thick black liquid sweetener with a caffeine-like kick.

Energy 178kcal/753kJ; Protein 2.3g; Carbohydrate 44g, of which sugars 44g; Fat 0.3g, of which saturates 0g; Cholesterol 0mg; Calcium 34mg; Fibre 3.8g; Sodium 5mg

Whole lime limeade

Limonada Suiça

Serves 2

1 ½ limes, washed and chopped

30ml/2 tbsp caster (superfine) sugar, or more to taste

500ml/17fl oz/2¼ cups water

250ml/8fl oz/1 cup ice cubes

If you've just spent the morning window shopping in the streets of Ipanema, in hot and humid Rio de Janeiro, you'll probably welcome refreshment at one of the many juice bars dotted around town. As thirst-quenchers go, this juice is in a class of its own. If there was a reason why it is called 'Swiss' limeade, it has long been forgotten.

1 Put the chopped limes, sugar, water and ice in a blender and blend for 2–3 minutes or until fairly smooth.

2 Sieve (strain), into a jug (pitcher) to remove the bits of skin and pith. Serve in tall glasses.

Pineapple and mint smoothie

Abacaxi com menta

Serves 2

1 large fresh ripe pineapple, about 300g/11oz, peeled and cut into chunks

30ml/2 tbsp caster (superfine) sugar (optional)

500ml/17fl oz/2¼ cups water, preferably chilled

25g/1oz/½ cup fresh mint leaves

250ml/8fl oz/1 cup ice cubes

September to December is pineapple-harvesting season in Brazil, and large open-backed lorries selling heavy loads of the ripe fruit park on the street corners of big cities all over the country. Brazilian bars make the most of this seasonal plenty by serving this non-alcoholic frothy pineapple and mint smoothie to thirsty customers.

1 Put the pineapple chunks, sugar, water, mint leaves, reserve a few to garnish, and ice in a blender. Blend for 3–4 minutes until smooth.

2 Pour the blended pineapple into tall glasses, topped with a little extra ice, if liked, decorate with mint leaves and serve each with a long-handled spoon.

Limeade: Energy 60kcal/258kJ; Protein 0.1g; Carbohydrate 16g, of which sugars 16g; Fat 0g, of which saturates 0g; Cholesterol 0mg; Calcium 3mg; Fibre 0g; Sodium 1mg
Pineapple: Energy 122kcal/521kJ; Protein 0.7g; Carbohydrate 31.1g, of which sugars 30.9g; Fat 0.3g, of which saturates 0g; Cholesterol 0mg; Calcium 35mg; Fibre 2g; Sodium 4mg

Lime and cachaça cocktail
Caipirinha

No home barbecue or party in Brazil is complete without caipirinhas. The cocktails, made as individual servings, are a simple blend of sugar, lime juice and cachaça – a distilled alcohol made from sugar cane. Serve with lots of ice.

Makes 1

- ½ lime
- 30ml/2 tbsp caster (superfine) sugar
- 250ml/8fl oz/1 cup crushed ice
- 50ml/2fl oz/¼ cup cachaça

1 Cut the lime into wedges and place in the glass, together with the sugar.

2 Use a cocktail muddler, or small rolling pin, to crush the lime and sugar together, releasing the oils from the lime skin and dissolving the sugar in the lime juice.

3 Top up the glass with the crushed ice, then pour in the cachaça. Stir and serve with straws.

Coconut cocktail
Batida de côco

Batidas are wonderful drinks to serve at a party or as appetizers before a meal, as they can be made well in advance and kept in a semi-frozen state until required to liven up your summer party. Smooth, silky, coconut batidas are the perfect start to a spicy meal.

1 Put the coconut milk, condensed milk, grated coconut and cachaça in a blender and blitz for one minute until smooth.

2 Pour into a large clean glass bottle, leaving a gap of at least 5cm/2in between the liquid and the top of the bottle. Close with a cork and chill in the refrigerator.

3 Place in the freezer for 1 hour before you are due to serve, to ensure your batida is icy cold.

Serves 12

- 400ml/14fl oz/1⅔ cups coconut milk
- 350ml/12fl oz/1½ cups condensed milk
- 115g/4oz/1 cup freshly grated coconut
- 300ml/½ pint/1¼ cups cachaça

Lime and cachaca: Energy 230kcal/967kJ; Protein 0g; Carbohydrate 31.7g, of which sugars 31.7g; Fat 0g; Cholesterol 0mg; Calcium 4mg; Fibre 0 g; Sodium 2mg
Coconut: Energy 194kcal/810kJ; Protein 2.9g; Carbohydrate 18.2g, of which sugars 18.2g; Fat 6.5g, of which saturates 4.9g; Cholesterol 11mg; Calcium 95mg; Fibre 1.2g; Sodium 79mg

Passion fruit cocktail

Batida de maracujá

Serves 12

400ml/14fl oz/1⅔ cups passion fruit concentrate

300ml/½ pint/1¼ cups cachaça

300ml/½ pint/1¼ cups water,

225g/8 oz/1 cup caster (superfine) sugar

pulp of 1 ripe passion fruit (optional)

A batida cocktail is a mix of cachaça and fruit juice. The secret of success is to introduce air in to the mix by either vigorous shaking or blending.

1 Put the passion fruit concentrate, cachaça, water and sugar in a blender and blend at high speed for a minute, until well mixed and slightly frothy. If using the fresh passion fruit, cut in half and scoop the pulp into the mix, blend for another minute, then strain the liquid through a sieve (strainer) into a jug (pitcher).

2 Pour into a glass bottle, leaving a 5cm/2in gap, seal with a cork and refrigerate. Place the bottle in the freezer 1 hour before serving, to make it icy cold.

Cashew apple fruit cocktail

Batida de cajú

Serves 12

400ml/14fl oz/1⅔ cups cajú fruit concentrate

300ml/½ pint/1¼ cups cachaça

300ml/½ pint/1¼ cups water

200g/7oz/scant 1 cup caster (superfine) sugar

Native to Brazil, cajú, or the cashew apple, is the delicious pear-shaped fruit that grows above the cashew nut. The juice is more popular than orange juice among locals, and is an opaque pale orange colour with a delicate, slightly astringent flavour. Like other batidas, because it is made in advance this is another great drink for a party.

1 Put all the ingredients in a blender and blend for one minute until smooth.

2 Pour into a glass bottle, to within 5cm/2in of the top, then seal with a cork and refrigerate.

3 Place the bottle in the freezer for 1 hour before serving to make it icy cold.

Passion fruit: Energy 87kcal/356kJ; Protein 0.5g; Carbohydrate 7.1g, of which sugars 7.1g; Fat 0.1g, of which saturates 0g; Cholesterol 0mg; Calcium 5mg; Fibre 0g; Sodium 13mg
Cashew: Energy 133kcal/561kJ; Protein 0.2g; Carbohydrate 20.4g, of which sugars 20.4g; Fat 0g, of which saturates 0g; Cholesterol 0mg; Calcium 5mg; Fibre 0g; Sodium 4mg

Fish and Seafood

With its long coastline and some of the largest rivers in the world, Brazil is a paradise for fish lovers, especially for those who appreciate the taste and texture of large freshwater fish.

Food from the oceans and rivers

Brazil's natives have used fish as their main source of protein for thousands of years. Once the Portuguese arrived, they were quick to incorporate local species into their diet as well.

Prawns (shrimp) are widely used in recipes brought by African slaves during the Portuguese colonization of Brazil, and have become popular throughout the country. Brazil is one of the world's biggest producers, and as a result prawns are a relatively inexpensive ingredient for delicious recipes such as Bobó de Camarão (prawns in cassava sauce), Vatapá (seafood and nut purée) or as a garnish for various types of moquecas (stews).

Octopus and squid are available at most fish markets all year round. Squid is a great substitute for fish in moquecas, and octopus is used in many seafood salads. It also features in the undeniably Portuguese-inspired dish, Polvo com Arroz de Bróccolis (octopus and broccoli rice).

A curious addition to the fish menu is Portuguese bacalhau (salt cod), which is not native to Brazil and is imported from Norway, making it an expensive yet popular delicacy. Brazilian cuisine has incorporated ancient Portuguese salt cod recipes with little or no alteration, and they are a popular choice for family celebrations.

Right middle: Some of the traditionally painted fishing boats of Brazil.
Page 45: A Brazilian fishing boat returns to harbour with its catch.

Stuffed baked crabs

Casquinha de siri

Crabs are plentiful in Brazil and can be found along its vast shoreline, long rivers and extensive marshlands. The 'siri' in the name of this dish refers to a large land crab mainly found in northern Brazil, and 'casquinha' refers to the crab shell that is traditionally used for serving. This dish is ideal for entertaining, especially if you use the crab shells instead of ramekins to bake it in.

Serves 8

- 2 slices day-old white bread
- 75ml/5 tbsp milk
- 15ml/1 tbsp olive oil
- 1 shallot, finely chopped
- 1 clove garlic, crushed
- 1 large tomato, peeled, seeded and chopped
- 90ml/6 tbsp white wine
- 45ml/3 tbsp butter, plus extra for greasing
- 450g/1lb white crab meat
- 15g/½oz/¼ cup chopped fresh coriander (cilantro)
- 5ml/1 tsp chopped parsley
- 1.5ml/¼ tsp grated nutmeg
- 2.5ml/½ tsp palm oil (dendê)
- 15ml/1 tbsp double (heavy) cream
- 65g/2½oz/generous ½ cup fine dry breadcrumbs
- 40g/1½oz/⅜ cup Parmesan cheese, grated
- wedges of lime and hot pepper sauce, to serve

1 Put the bread on a shallow plate or in a small bowl and spoon over the milk. Leave to soak for a few minutes. Lightly grease eight clean, empty crab shells, scallop shells or shallow ramekins with butter.

2 Heat the olive oil in a pan over a medium heat. Add the shallot and fry for 2 minutes until soft. Add the garlic and fry for another minute.

3 Add the tomato and white wine to the pan, and bring to the boil. Reduce the heat and gently simmer for 5 minutes. Remove from the heat and set aside to cool.

4 Take the bread out of the milk, and squeeze it dry, then crumble it with your fingers and stir it into the tomato sauce.

5 Melt the butter over a medium heat and fry the crab meat for a few seconds. Add the tomato sauce, coriander, parsley, nutmeg and palm oil. Simmer for 2 minutes, or until the mixture has little visible liquid, but is still moist. Turn off the heat, then stir in the cream.

6 Preheat the oven to 200°C/400°F/Gas 6. In a small bowl, mix together the breadcrumbs and grated Parmesan.

7 Spoon the crab mixture into the shells or ramekins and smooth the tops with the back of a spoon. Sprinkle over the Parmesan and breadcrumb mixture, and bake for 10 minutes until the tops are golden.

8 Serve straight away, accompanied by lime wedges to squeeze over and hot pepper sauce.

Energy 208kcal/869kJ; Protein 12.6g; Carbohydrate 12g, of which sugars 1.7g; Fat 12.5g, of which saturates 5.5g; Cholesterol 52mg; Calcium 89mg; Fibre 1.1g; Sodium 420mg

Octopus and broccoli rice

Polvo com arroz de brócolis

Unlike squid, octopus requires very long cooking to ensure it is tender, and here a pressure cooker is recommended to shorten the time required. Surprisingly, freezing can also tenderize octopus, so if you can, buy it a few days before you need it and freeze, then thaw it in the refrigerator overnight.

Serves 6–8

- 600g/1lb 6oz octopus tentacles
- 60ml/4 tbsp olive oil
- ½ onion, chopped
- 5 cloves garlic, finely chopped
- 5ml/1 tsp white peppercorns, finely crushed
- 1 large tomato, peeled, seeded and chopped
- 250ml/8fl oz/1 cup dry white wine
- 350g/12oz broccoli florets
- 400g/14oz/4 cups White Rice (see page 84)
- 20g/¾oz/⅓ cup fresh parsley, chopped
- salt
- lime wedges, hot pepper sauce, Brazilian Salsa (see page 96), toasted French bread and olive oil, to serve

Cook's tip If you don't have a pressure cooker use a large pan in step 3. Increase the cooking time to 1 hour.

1 Wash the octopus tentacles thoroughly in a large bowl of cold water. Trim off the very thin tips of the tentacles.

2 Heat 30ml/2 tbsp of the oil in a pressure cooker and fry the onion for 8–10 minutes until soft, but not browned. Add a third of the garlic and fry for 1 minute. Add the octopus and the white peppercorns and fry for 1 minute, then add the chopped tomato, white wine and just enough water to cover the octopus.

3 Close the pressure cooker, bring to pressure point, reduce the heat and cook for 15 minutes, following the manufacturer's instructions.

4 Open the cooker, remove the lid, and leave the octopus to cool in the stock.

5 Meanwhile, add the broccoli to a large pan of boiling salted water and cook for 3–5 minutes until just tender. Drain, and when cool enough to handle, chop into tiny florets.

6 Remove the octopus from the liquid in the pressure cooker and cut into 2cm/¾in slices.

7 In a large pan or wok, heat the remaining 30ml/2 tbsp olive oil and fry the remaining garlic until it starts to brown, then add the broccoli florets.

8 Add the octopus, the stock from the pressure cooker, rice and salt to taste. Stir to mix thoroughly and continue to cook for 4–5 minutes, until piping hot.

9 Transfer to a warm serving plate and garnish with parsley. Serve with lime wedges, hot pepper sauce, Brazilian Salsa, toasted French bread and a bowl of olive oil.

Energy 153kcal; 639kJ; Protein 15.8g; Carbohydrate 2.4g, of which sugars 1.8g; Fat 9g, of which saturates 1.4g; Cholesterol 36mg; Calcium 56mg; Fibre 0.5g; Sodium 89mg

Prawns in cassava sauce

Bobó de camarão

Bobó is the name given to any dish thickened with cassava. Its origins lie in West Africa, where it is made with yam; the recipe was brought to Brazil by slaves. Cassava is used extensively in Brazilian cooking in preference to potatoes, rice and pasta. It mashes to a wonderfully smooth purée which here is turned into a sauce with the addition of creamy coconut milk, tomatoes and a tasty stock.

1 Place the prawns in a bowl, add the lime juice, garlic, salt and pepper. Mix, then set aside to marinate for about 20 minutes.

2 Put the prawn heads and shells in a pan and add water to just cover. Slowly bring to the boil, reduce the heat and gently simmer for 20–30 minutes. Strain the stock and set aside.

3 Meanwhile, peel the cassava root and cut into three or four large chunks. Put in a large pan and cover with water. Stud the onion with cloves and add to the pan with the bay leaves. Bring to the boil, lower the heat, half-cover with a lid and simmer for 20 minutes, until tender.

4 Drain the cassava, keeping the onion. When the cassava is cool enough to handle, remove and discard the ropey fibres from the middle. Chop the flesh into cubes, return to the pan, then mash, gradually adding the coconut milk.

5 Heat the oil in a clean pan over a high heat. Remove the prawns from the marinade and add to the pan, reserving the marinade.

6 Briefly fry the prawns until almost cooked through. Remove them from the pan, leaving most of the oil behind, and set aside.

7 Remove the cloves from the onion, roughly chop the onion and add to the pan. Cook over a high heat for 2–3 minutes, then add any remaining marinade and cook for a further 2–3 minutes. Add the tomatoes and tomato purée and 250ml/8fl oz/1 cup of the prawn stock. Reduce the heat and simmer for 5 minutes.

8 Remove the pan from the heat and with a hand-held blender, or a wooden spoon, gradually add the cassava mash to the tomato sauce. If using a wooden spoon, vigorously beat the two together.

9 Check the seasoning and add more salt and pepper if needed. Add the prawns and cream and cook for a further 2–3 minutes to finish cooking the prawns and to heat through. Remove from the heat and stir in the palm oil and coriander. Transfer to a warmed serving dish and serve piping hot, with steamed rice.

Serves 6

- 800g/1¾lb large raw prawns (shrimp) peeled, shells retained, and de-veined
- juice of 1 lime
- 6 cloves garlic, crushed
- 2.5-5ml/½–1 tsp salt
- 2.5-5ml/½–1 tsp ground black pepper
- 600g/1lb 6oz cassava root
- 1 onion
- 6 cloves
- 2 bay leaves
- 300ml/½ pint/1¼ cups coconut milk
- 60ml/4 tbsp vegetable oil
- 6 large tomatoes, peeled, seeded and chopped
- 15ml/1 tbsp tomato purée (paste)
- 45ml/3 tbsp double (heavy) cream
- 30ml/2 tbsp palm oil (dendê)
- 25g/1oz/½ cup coriander (cilantro), chopped

Energy 466kcal/1959kJ; Protein 26.1g; Carbohydrate 46.9g, of which sugars 10.6g; Fat 20.7g, of which saturates 6.5g; Cholesterol 270mg; Calcium 163mg; Fibre 4.0g; Sodium 500mg

Seafood and nut purée

Vatapá

This is a classic dish from the Bahia region of Brazil. It can be eaten as a main course or more usually as an accompaniment; a thicker version is good as a filling for Acarajé (black-eyed bean fritters). Vatapá may have originated in Portugal, but the use of ground nuts, coconut milk and palm oil place it firmly on the Brazilian menu.

1 Tear the bread in small pieces and place in a bowl. Pour over the milk and set aside to soak.

2 Meanwhile, heat the stock in a medium pan, add the fish and poach for 3–5 minutes, depending on the thickness of the fillets, until just cooked. Remove the fish with a slotted spoon and place on a board or plate. Reserve the stock. When the fish fillets are cool enough to handle, flake and set aside.

3 Put the dried shrimp, peanuts and cashews in a food processor and blend until fine. Squeeze the bread dry and add to the processor with the fish. Blend again to a smooth purée.

4 Spoon and scrape the purée into a pan and gradually add enough of the stock to achieve a creamy consistency (you won't need it all). Add the ginger and nutmeg and season with salt and pepper to taste.

5 Cook for 3–4 minutes over a medium heat, then reduce to a simmer, stirring constantly, for 10 minutes until it becomes very thick.

6 Stir in the lime juice and palm oil, and cook for another 2 minutes, then add the coconut milk and hot pepper sauce, and cook for a further 3 or 4 minutes. Spoon into a bowl and garnish with cooked prawns and lime wedges.

Serves 8

- ½ loaf day-old French bread
- 500ml/17fl oz/2¼ cups milk
- 750ml/1¼ pints/3 cups fish stock
- 450g/1lb white fish fillets
- 65g/2½ oz dried shrimp
- 75g/3oz/¾ cup roasted unsalted peanuts
- 75g/3oz/¾ cup roasted cashews
- 2.5ml/½ tsp fresh root ginger, grated
- 1.5ml/¼ tsp ground nutmeg
- 30ml/2 tbsp lime juice
- 15ml/1 tbsp palm oil (dendê)
- 200ml/7fl oz/scant 1 cup coconut milk
- 5ml/1 tsp hot pepper sauce
- salt and ground black pepper
- large cooked prawns (shrimp), and lime wedges to garnish

Energy 302/1268kJ; Protein 15.3g; Carbohydrate 32.5g, of which sugars 6.7g; Fat 13.2g, of which saturates 3.4g; Cholesterol 45mg; Calcium 245mg; Fibre 2.7g; Sodium 878mg

Fish stew in coconut milk

Moqueca baiana

Serves 6

60ml/4 tbsp vegetable oil

1 red and 1 green (bell) pepper, cut into rings

1 large onion, cut into rings

1 red chilli pepper (optional), seeded and cut into rings

2 cloves garlic, chopped

2 large tomatoes, chopped

15ml/1 tbsp tomato purée (paste)

6 spring onions (scallions), finely sliced

1kg/2¼lb firm white fish fillets such as red snapper or monkfish cut into slices

12 large raw prawns (shrimp), shelled and deveined

400ml/14fl oz/1⅔ cups coconut milk

30ml/2 tbsp palm oil (dendê)

salt and ground black pepper

coriander (cilantro) sprigs, to garnish

The term 'moqueca' comes from the Tupi word 'moquem', a method used by native Brazilians to cook meat and fish by wrapping it in leaves and grilling it over a fire. This technique evolved into cooking in a pot over the fire, and eventually to stewing on a stove. This recipe, popular in Bahia and Rio de Janeiro, uses white fish, but prawn, squid or crab can be used. Serve with Brazilian-style white rice if you wish.

1 Heat the oil in a deep frying pan or shallow pan and fry the red and green peppers and onion for 3–4 minutes. Add the red chilli (if using) and garlic, and fry for another minute.

2 Add the tomatoes, tomato purée and spring onions to the pan. Season with salt and black pepper. Lower the heat, cover the pan, and gently cook, stirring frequently, for 5 minutes.

3 Add the fish fillets to the mixture. Cook for 2 minutes, then add the prawns, and cook for a further 2 minutes, stirring occasionally.

4 Finally, add the coconut milk and palm oil to the pan, turn up the heat a little and let it bubble for one minute. Remove from the heat, garnish with coriander sprigs, and serve with Brazilian-style white rice (see page 84).

Energy 363kcal/1522kJ; Protein 41g; Carbohydrate 10.4g, of which sugars 9.2g; Fat 17.9g, of which saturates 4.3g; Cholesterol 135mg; Calcium 153mg; Fibre 1.9g; Sodium 352mg

Salt cod and potatoes

Bacalhau à Gomes de Sá

The Portuguese refer to salt cod as their 'faithful friend', and famously have a different recipe for every day of the year. It was an obvious choice as a non-perishable food for the three month-long voyages across the Atlantic to Brazil, although why it was so readily adopted by a country with vast supplies of fresh fish has more to do with fashion and religion. Most Brazilian restaurants have at least one bacalhau dish on the menu, and it is often a version of this recipe, created by Gomes de Sá at his restaurant in Porto.

Serves 6

- 500g/1¼lb bacalhau (salt cod)
- 500g/1¼lb medium-sized potatoes
- 1 litre/1¾ pints/4 cups milk
- 1 bay leaf
- 150ml/¼ pint/⅔ cup olive oil
- 2 onions, sliced into rings
- 2 cloves garlic, sliced
- 175g/6oz/1 cup black olives
- freshly ground white pepper
- 45ml/3 tbsp fresh parsley, chopped, and 2 hard-boiled eggs, sliced, to garnish
- green salad and crusty bread, to serve

Cook's tip Use a waxy, yellow-fleshed variety of potato, that won't disintegrate during cooking.

1 Place the cod in a large bowl with plenty of water, and soak for 24–36 hours, changing the water at least three times.

2 Drain the cod, put in a large pan and add enough boiling water to come about 5cm/2in above the fish. Gently simmer for 20 minutes, then carefully remove the pieces of cod and set aside to cool. Keep the stock in the pan.

3 When cool enough to handle, remove any bones and skin, then flake the fish into bitesize chunks and put in a bowl.

4 Heat the milk and bay leaf until nearly boiling and pour over the fish. Leave to infuse for at least 2 hours.

5 Add the potatoes to the fish stock and bring back to the boil. Half-cover with a pan lid and simmer for 20 minutes, until tender. Drain, and when cool enough to handle, peel and cut the potatoes into 1cm/½in thick slices.

6 Transfer the cod into a colander and leave for a few minutes until well drained. Preheat the oven to 200°C/400°F/Gas 6.

7 Heat the oil in a large shallow pan and add the onions and the garlic. Gently cook for 2–3 minutes, then add the potato slices, the cod flakes and the black olives.

8 Mix together, taking care to not flake the cod further or break too many of the potato slices. Season with freshly ground white pepper, cover and simmer for 3–4 minutes.

9 Transfer the fish mixture, sauteéd onions and potatoes to a deep ceramic dish, making sure the potatoes are flat. Drizzle any olive oil left in the pan over the top. Bake for 10 minutes.

10 Remove from the oven and garnish with the chopped parsley and slices of hard-boiled egg. Serve the salt cod and potatoes with a simple green salad and crusty bread.

Energy 551kcal/2292kJ; Protein 35.1g; Carbohydrate 26.2g, of which sugars 11.2g; Fat 34.1g, of which saturates 6.5g; Cholesterol 87mg; Calcium 437mg; Fibre 3.4g; Sodium 4372mg

Leão Veloso fish soup

Sopa Leão Veloso

This delicious soup is named after Leão Veloso, a Brazilian ambassador to France who was famous for his love of the arts and his appreciation of good food. He is credited with adapting the French dish, bouillabaisse, into this Brazilian version, using local seafood and spices.

1 Rinse the mussels under cold running water to help rid them of any grit, then scrub the shells to remove any barnacles. Pull off any hairy 'beards' which protrude from the side of the shell. Tap any open mussels sharply with the back of a knife. If they don't close, throw them away.

2 Shell and devein the prawns, keeping the heads and shells. Clean and fillet the fish (or ask the fishmonger to do this for you), keeping the heads and the trimmings, then cut the fillets into chunks.

3 Put the prawn shells, fish heads and trimmings in a large pan, then pour over 2.25 litres/4 pints/10 cups cold water. Add the sprigs of parsley and coriander and the bay leaf. Slowly bring to boiling point, then gently simmer uncovered for 1 hour, skimming the surface occasionally, to make a stock.

4 Pour the stock through a fine sieve (strainer) or a muslin-lined colander into a bowl. Discard the prawn and fish trimmings and herbs.

5 Rinse out the pan, return the stock to it and continue to simmer. Add the tomatoes, chopped parsley and spring onions and cook for 5 minutes.

6 Crush the coriander seeds in a spice grinder or with a mortar and pestle. Add the garlic and 5ml/1 tsp salt and grind or crush into a paste, then add to the stock.

7 Heat the oil in a deep frying pan and fry the fish and prawns until golden. Add a ladleful of the stock to the frying pan, and stir to deglaze and lift all the juices, then transfer the fish and liquid to the stock.

8 Add the crab meat, lobster meat and mussels to the stock and cook for 5 minutes or until the mussels open. Remove any mussels that remain closed.

9 Taste and season the soup with a little more salt, if necessary, and plenty of ground black pepper. Ladle into warmed bowls and serve straight away with some bread.

Serves 6–8

1 kg/2¼lb fresh mussels

300g/11oz raw tiger prawns (jumbo shrimp), unpeeled

1kg/2¼lb whole white fish, such as grouper, sea bass, snapper or tilapia

25g/1oz/½ cup fresh parsley sprigs, plus 30ml/2 tbsp finely chopped

25g/1oz/½ cup fresh coriander (cilantro) sprigs

1 bay leaf

400g/14oz tomatoes, peeled, seeded and chopped

6 spring onions (scallions), roughly chopped

5ml/1 tsp coriander seeds

2 cloves garlic

30ml/2 tbsp olive oil

300g/11oz white crab meat

300g/11oz cooked lobster meat

salt and ground black pepper

crusty bread, to serve

Energy 367kcal/1545kJ; Protein 62.6g; Carbohydrate 5.5g, of which sugars 2.2g; Fat 10.7g, of which saturates 1.8g; Cholesterol 239mg; Calcium 178mg; Fibre 0.9g; Sodium 883mg

Meat and Poultry

Brazilians are habitual carnivores and most of them would not consider a meal complete unless it contained some form of meat, often in hearty portions.

Best quality produce from the market

Beef, chicken and pork are by far the most popular meats in Brazil. Lamb is very rarely eaten, and most of the lamb for sale has been imported, making it very expensive.

Brazilian beef is considered as the best in the world. It comes mainly from the south, from the wide grassy plains of the Pampas near the frontier with Argentina and Paraguay. Fillet steak is as costly as in any other country, but Brazilians are happy to replace it with picanha (best rump with a layer of fat) in most recipes, such as Picadinho à Carioca (beef stew). Picanha is especially good for grilling, as its blanket of fat keeps the cut moist. Cheaper cuts, like oxtail, are used in Rabada com Agrião (oxtail stew and watercress).

Pork is famously associated with State of Minas Gerais, in the east, where several regional recipes call for pork loin or chops. Owing to a great influx of Italian and German immigrants, Minas Gerais also became famous for the production of cured pork and tasty sausages.

During the years of colonization, cured beef helped the Portuguese explorers on long journeys through the country. Carne seca (beef jerky) is still a favourite ingredient, especially in the north-east in dishes like Jabá com Jerimum (beef jerky and pumpkin). It is best used in small quantities, as it has a very strong flavour.

Right middle: A restaurant in Sao Paulo.
Page 61: A cattle drive in South Para State, Amazon, Brazil.

Chicken and prawn stew

Xinxim de galinha

Cooking chicken on the bone adds to the final flavour of this delicious dish. Tangy lime and spicy ginger are mellowed by creamy coconut, then fresh green peppers and tomatoes are added to the sauce – all typical ingredients of classic Brazilian cuisine. Serve with rice and Golden Farofa.

Serves 6

- 3 limes
- 4 cloves garlic, crushed
- 60ml/4 tbsp vegetable oil
- 1.6kg/3½lb chicken, jointed
- 350g/12oz raw tiger prawns (jumbo shrimp)
- 1 large onion, finely chopped
- 1 large green (bell) pepper, seeded and chopped
- 4 plum tomatoes, peeled, seeded and chopped
- 450ml/¾ pint/scant 2 cups chicken stock
- 40g/1½oz dried shrimp
- 40g/1½oz piece fresh root ginger, peeled and grated
- 25g/1oz/¼ cup cashew nuts
- 25g/1oz/¼ cup roasted unsalted peanuts
- 30ml/2 tbsp palm oil (dendê)
- 400ml/14fl oz/1¾ cups coconut milk
- 25g/1oz/½ cup of chopped fresh coriander (cilantro)
- salt and ground black pepper

1 Whisk together the juice of 1 lime, a third of the garlic, 15ml/1 tbsp of the oil, salt and pepper in a large bowl. Add the chicken pieces and turn until coated in the mixture. Leave to marinate for at least 20 minutes.

2 Peel and devein the tiger prawns, then marinate in the juice of 1 lime, a third of the garlic, salt and pepper, for about 15 minutes.

3 Heat 15ml/1 tbsp of the oil in a large frying pan over a high heat. Add the prawns and stir-fry for 2 minutes, until just pink, but not quite cooked through. Remove and set aside.

4 Add 15ml/1 tbsp more oil to the frying pan and fry the chicken, turning frequently until golden on all sides. Remove and set aside.

5 Add the remaining 15ml/1 tbsp oil to the pan and fry the onion until soft, but not browned. Add the green pepper and the rest of the garlic and fry for 1 minute. Then add the tomatoes, chicken pieces and stock and bring to the boil. Lower the heat, cover the pan and gently simmer for 30 minutes.

6 Meanwhile, in a small food processor, or with a mortar and pestle, finely grind the dried shrimp, ginger, cashew nuts and peanuts. Add to the pan and simmer for a further 5 minutes.

7 Stir in the cooked prawns, palm oil and coconut milk, then simmer for a final 3–4 minutes, or until the chicken is tender. Adjust the seasoning, if necessary. Sprinkle with fresh coriander and serve hot, accompanied by White Rice (page 84) and Golden Farofa (page 94).

Energy 419kcal/1751kJ; Protein 41.9g; Carbohydrate 10.4g, of which sugars 8.5g; Fat 23.7g, of which saturates 5.9g; Cholesterol 253mg; Calcium 190mg; Fibre 2g; Sodium 808mg

Chicken and palm hearts pie

Pastelão de frango e palmito

Palm hearts are harvested from the soft core of the palm tree and are extremely popular in Brazilian cooking. They can be eaten raw or cooked. Even in Brazil it is difficult to obtain fresh palm hearts, and when available they are very expensive, so this dish is usually made with canned ones.

Serves 6

For the filling:

- 700g/1½lb skinless chicken breast portions
- 4 cloves garlic, crushed
- 60ml/4 tbsp vegetable oil
- 1 onion, chopped
- 4 tomatoes, peeled and seeded
- 300g/11oz drained canned palm hearts, chopped
- 30ml/2 tbsp fresh parsley, chopped
- 4 spring onions (scallions), finely chopped
- salt and ground black pepper

For the shortcrust pastry:

- 850g/1lb 14oz/7½ cups plain (all-purpose) flour
- 10ml/2 tsp salt
- 300g/11oz lard or butter, or half and half of each
- 2 egg yolks
- 1 egg yolk and 5ml/1 tsp olive oil, to glaze

1 Chop the chicken breasts into small cubes and place in a bowl. Add the crushed garlic, season with salt and pepper, mix well and leave to marinate for 20 minutes.

2 To make the pastry, sift the flour and salt into a large bowl. Rub in the fat with your fingers until the mixture resembles fine breadcrumbs. Mix in the egg yolks, and enough water to form a dough. Gather into a ball, and knead on a floured surface until smooth. Wrap in clear film (plastic wrap) and chill for 30 minutes.

3 Meanwhile, make the filling. Heat the oil in a large frying pan and fry the onion for 5 minutes, until beginning to soften. Add the chicken and continue to fry for 4–5 minutes, stirring. Add the tomatoes, palm hearts, parsley and spring onions and cook for a further 5 minutes. Season with salt and pepper, then remove from the heat and set aside to cool.

4 Put a baking sheet in the oven and preheat it to 190°C/375°F/Gas 5. Remove the pastry from the refrigerator and cut into two pieces, one slightly larger than the other.

5 Roll out the bigger piece on a floured surface until big enough to line a 23cm/9in square cake tin (pan). Ease the pastry in gently, leaving a small amount overhanging the edges (this will be trimmed later). Line with baking parchment and ceramic baking beads or dried beans, spreading them out evenly to cover the base. Put on the hot baking sheet in the oven and bake for 20 minutes.

6 Remove the pastry case from the oven and lift out the baking parchment and beans. Allow the pastry to cool for 5 minutes. Then add the filling, spreading it evenly.

7 Roll out the second piece of pastry and place on top of the filling. Trim the excess pastry with a knife, cutting off the part-cooked pastry too, and press down around the edges to seal. Decorate the top with the trimmings, if you like.

8 In a small bowl, mix the egg yolk and the olive oil and brush thinly over the top. Pierce a few small holes in the pastry lid to let any steam escape. Bake for 30 minutes or until the crust is golden brown. Serve in slices, warm or cold.

Energy 1167kcal/4885kJ; Protein 44.3g; Carbohydrate 114.2g, of which sugars 5g; Fat 62.4g, of which saturates 25.9g; Cholesterol 259mg; Calcium 244mg; Fibre 7g; Sodium 954mg

Oxtail stew with watercress

Rabada com agrião

Oxtail has a wonderful rich flavour and really benefits from lengthy, moist slow cooking. This stew is extremely popular in Brazil, and a yardstick to measure the quality of any restaurant claiming to serve authentic Brazilian food. The sauce gains an almost gelatinous texture from the bones as it cooks, and the fresh peppery taste of watercress perfectly balances the richness of the meat.

Serves 4

- 1 onion, roughly chopped
- 4 cloves garlic
- 45ml/3 tbsp olive oil
- 250ml/8fl oz/1 cup dry white wine
- 2 small oxtails, about 1.5kg/3lb weight in total
- 30ml/2 tbsp vegetable oil
- 2 large tomatoes, peeled, seeded and finely chopped
- 2 bay leaves
- 250ml/8fl oz/1 cup cold water
- 5ml/1 tsp cornflour (cornstarch)
- 2 large bunches watercress, washed
- salt and ground black pepper
- creamy or fried polenta, to serve

Variation If you are unable to find watercress, use rocket (arugula) instead.

1 Make a marinade by puréeing the onion, garlic, olive oil and a little salt and pepper in a blender or food processor. Add a little of the wine if you need more liquid, to help it blend to a smooth purée. Transfer to a large bowl and stir in the rest of the wine.

2 Trim the oxtails, rinse under cold running water, then pat dry. Cut into large pieces about 5cm/2in thick with a sharp knife or a cleaver (your butcher may already have done this). Add to the marinade and mix well to ensure all pieces are coated. Cover and leave in the refrigerator to marinate for at least 4 and up to 12 hours. Remove from the marinade, brushing off the residue. Reserve the marinade.

3 Heat the vegetable oil in a pressure cooker over a high heat. Add the oxtail and fry, in batches if necessary, until browned on all sides. Add the tomatoes and cook for 2 minutes.

4 Add the marinade and the bay leaves, and stir well. Bring to the boil and add the water.

5 Close the pressure cooker. Following the manufacturer's instructions, cook the stew for 30 minutes; the oxtail should be very tender and almost falling off the bone.

6 Blend the cornflour to a thin paste with 100ml/3½fl oz/scant ½ cup of cold water. Gradually add this to the meat and sauce, stirring it in gently, then let the mixture bubble for a further 5 minutes.

7 Remove the pan from the heat, top the stew with the fresh watercress and cover with the lid to keep warm. Leave it for 5 minutes so that the watercress wilts.

8 Serve the stew on a bed of creamy polenta, or alongside fried polenta fingers, topped by the wilted watercress.

Cook's tip If you don't own a pressure cooker, use a heavy pan and gently simmer the oxtail for 3–4 hours over a low heat, adding a little more water, if needed.

Energy 663kcal/2760kJ; Protein 59.2g; Carbohydrate 7g, of which sugars 4.6g; Fat 44.4g, of which saturates 2.6g; Cholesterol 206mg; Calcium 84mg; Fibre 2.3g; Sodium 475mg

Fillet steak with crunchy garlic topping

Filé Oswaldo Aranha

Serves 1

15ml/1 tbsp vegetable oil

1 fillet steak, about 400g/14oz

3 cloves of garlic, chopped

75g/3oz/scant ⅓ cup butter

salt and ground black pepper

sautéed or chipped potatoes or rice, and Brazilian-style Shredded Greens (see page 90), to serve

When Rio de Janeiro was Brazil's capital, so many government ministers ate at the Cosmopolita restaurant that it became known as 'The Little Senate'. One politician, Oswaldo Aranha, always ordered a thick fillet steak covered in toasted garlic. This was later incorporated into the restaurant's menu and is now popular all over Rio.

1 Heat the oil in a frying pan over a high heat. Add the steak and fry on both sides until medium-rare, or done to your liking. Transfer to a warm plate and leave to rest.

2 Wipe the frying pan clean with kitchen paper and return to a medium heat. Add the butter, and let it melt completely, then add the garlic.

3 Watch the garlic carefully as it burns easily, and remove it from the pan as soon as it turns a rich golden colour.

4 Spoon the garlic and butter over the fillet steak. Serve straight away together with sautéed or chipped potatoes and Brazilian-style Shredded Greens.

Energy 1020kcal/4235kJ; Protein 85.8g; Carbohydrate 1.7g, of which sugars 0.4g; Fat 74.4g, of which saturates 35.1g; Cholesterol 335mg; Calcium 25mg; Fibre 0 g; Sodium 827mg

Beef stew

Picadinho à carioca

Rio de Janeiro is the second largest city in Brazil. It is the cultural hub of the country and birthplace of the 'Bossa Nova' style of Brazilian music. This simple stew matches the fast and hectic lifestyle of those who live in the city. It is a quick and easy dish that relies on a tender cut of beef.

1 Cut the steak into 1cm/½in cubes and put in a bowl. Add the garlic and some black pepper, and leave the flavours to mingle for 30 minutes.

2 Meanwhile, heat the oil in a frying pan over a high heat and add the bacon lardons, fry for 2–3 minutes, or until the fat starts to run.

3 Add the beef to the pan and fry for 3–4 minutes, turning the pieces until they start to brown, then add the onion. Continue frying until the bacon and beef are browned and the onion is soft. Add the beef stock, lower the heat and simmer for 5 minutes.

4 Meanwhile, half-fill a pan with boiling water, add the vinegar and a pinch of salt and bring back to the boil. Switch off the heat and stir the water until it creates a slow swirl. Crack the eggs one at a time into the centre of the swirl. Let each egg poach for 2 minutes, then use a slotted spoon to transfer it to a plate.

5 Blend the cornflour with 15ml/1 tbsp of cold water and stir it into the beef. Cook, stirring, until the sauce thickens. Stir in the parsley, taste and season if needed. Ladle the beef into warmed bowls, and top with an egg. Serve with Deep-fried Straw Potatoes (see page 91).

Serves 2

- 400g/14oz fillet steak
- 2 cloves garlic, crushed
- 30ml/2 tbsp vegetable oil
- 125g/4½ oz bacon lardons
- 1 small onion, chopped
- 400ml/14fl oz/1¾ cups beef stock
- 30ml/2 tbsp white wine vinegar
- 2 eggs
- 5ml/1 tsp cornflour (cornstarch)
- 15ml/1 tbsp parsley, chopped
- salt and ground black pepper

Energy 700kcal/2911kJ; Protein 61.3g; Carbohydrate 5.2g, of which sugars 1.8g; Fat 48.9g, of which saturates 14.5g; Cholesterol 394mg; Calcium 61mg; Fibre 0.6g; Sodium 1670mg

Beef jerky and pumpkin

Jabá com jerimum

This recipe is from the state of Pernambuco, in the north-east of Brazil, where they have their own weird and wonderful names for different foods. The dry, hot weather makes the region an ideal place to produce beef jerky, and it is often used in local dishes. Locally grown pumpkins add colour and a distinctive sweet taste to the dish; they are the perfect partner for the gamey flavour of beef jerky.

Serves 6

- 500g/1¼lb beef jerky
- 1kg/2¼lb pumpkin or butternut squash, peeled and seeded
- 30ml/2 tbsp vegetable oil
- 1 large onion, thinly sliced
- 2 cloves garlic, crushed
- 25g/1oz/½ cup chopped fresh parsley
- ground black pepper
- White Rice Brazilian-style (see page 84), and hot pepper sauce, to serve

1 Cut the beef jerky into 5cm/2 in chunks. Put in a pan, cover with plenty of cold water and bring to the boil. Turn down the heat a little and simmer for 1 hour, or until tender. During this time, change the water 3 times to help remove most of the salt.

2 Lift out the pieces of jerky from the water and set aside to cool. Reserve the last pan of cooking water. When cool enough to handle, shred the beef with your hands, removing any bits of sinew.

3 While the jerky is cooking, cut the pumpkin into 2.5cm/1in cubes. Add them to the reserved water from cooking the jerky, adding more water if needed to cover. Bring to the boil, lower the heat and simmer for 10–12 minutes, until tender. Drain and set aside.

4 Meanwhile, heat the oil in a large frying pan and fry the onion for 8–10 minutes until soft.

5 Add the garlic and fry for another minute, then add the shredded beef jerky.

6 Fry for 3–4 minutes, using a spoon to break down the jerky into a fine straw-like fibre.

7 Stir the cooked pumpkin into the beef, then sprinkle with the chopped parsley and season with salt (if needed) and ground black pepper. Heat for 2 more minutes or until piping hot. Serve with White Rice Brazilian-style and hot pepper sauce.

Cook's tip Taste the beef jerky after each stage of boiling to ensure that enough salt has been removed, and taste the dish before adding more salt in step 5.

Energy 1002kcal/4241kJ; Protein 29.7g; Carbohydrate 169.8g, of which sugars 10.4g; Fat 26.9g, of which saturates 9.8g; Cholesterol 40mg; Calcium 85mg; Fibre 2.7g; Sodium 1744mg

Beef jerky risotto

Arroz de carreteiro

A carreteiro was a wagon master who transported goods across the vast grasslands of the southern states of Brazil. His need for a hot meal that was easy to prepare and made from long-lasting ingredients created a recipe that would become synonymous with the profession and a symbol of the state of Rio Grande do Sul. The original recipe called for little more than onions, charque (a kind of beef jerky produced in the south of Brazil) and rice, but extra ingredients have been added over time.

Serves 6–8

500g/1¼lb beef jerky

45ml/3 tbsp vegetable oil

115g/4oz bacon lardons

1 onion, finely chopped

3 cloves garlic, finely chopped

65g/2½oz smoked pork sausage such as kabanos, chouriço or chorizo

375g/13oz/generous 1½ cups easy-cook white rice

1 red chilli, seeded and very finely chopped

30ml/2 tbsp fresh parsley, chopped

2 spring onions (scallions), chopped

ground black pepper

Cook's tip If you can't find beef jerky, use other pieces of cured or cooked meat, such as leftovers from a barbecue or the Sunday joint.

1 Cut the beef jerky into 1cm/½in cubes. Place in a medium pan and cover with water. Bring to the boil, lower the heat and simmer for 45 minutes to 1 hour, replacing the water three times to remove excess salt.

2 In a large pan or casserole dish, heat the oil and fry the bacon lardons for one minute, then add the sliced onion and fry for 2 minutes more until starting to soften. Add the chopped garlic and fry for 1 more minute, stirring all the time.

3 Cut the smoked pork sausage into 1cm/½in cubes and add to the pan, together with the pre-cooked beef jerky, and fry, stirring, for a further 2 minutes.

4 Add the rice and cook for a few seconds, stirring everything together. Add enough boiling water to cover the ingredients by 2.5cm/1in and bring to the boil. Reduce the heat and cover the pan. Simmer the risotto for 15–20 minutes, or until the rice is tender and has absorbed all the liquid.

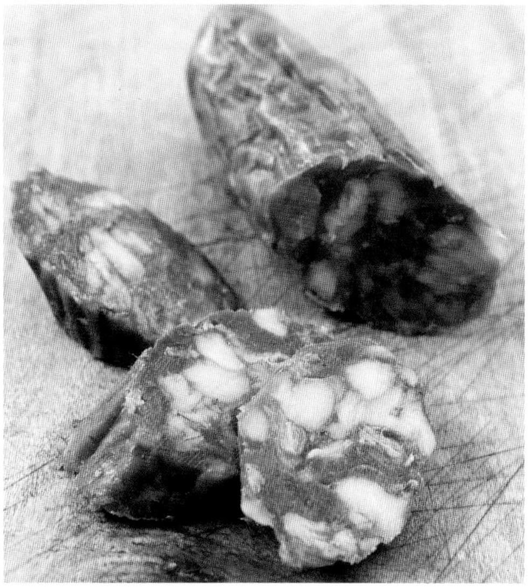

5 If the rice is not quite tender and there is no more liquid, add a few more tablespoons of just-boiled water and simmer for 2–3 minutes more until cooked.

6 Stir the chilli, parsley and spring onions into the rice. Taste and season with pepper. Serve straight away.

Energy 485kcal/2055kJ; Protein 5.5g; Carbohydrate 101g, of which sugars 1.4g; Fat 9.3g, of which saturates 1.9g; Cholesterol 0mg; Calcium 63mg; Fibre 1.6g; Sodium 52mg

Grilled rump steak

Picanha fatiada

In Brazil's famous steakhouses, the churrascarias, picanha is one of the most sought-after cuts, cooked over the barbecue, then served in slices. True Picanha aficionados prefer it served as a thick steak, seasoned with nothing but salt.

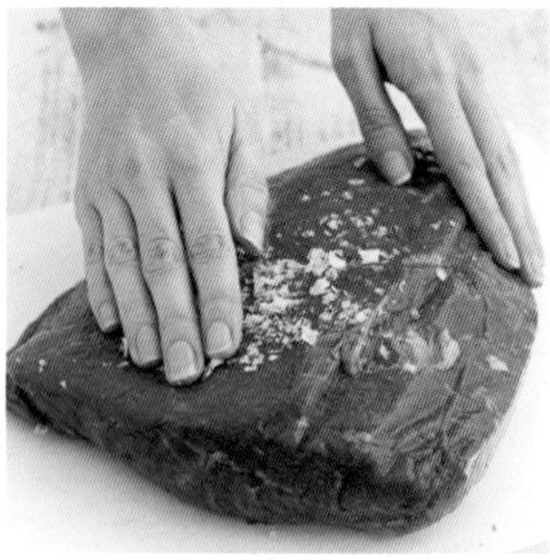

1 Rub the salt all over the beef, massaging it in. Leave at room temperature for 30 minutes.

2 Place the meat on a board, with the fat facing down and the narrower point of the triangular joint towards you. Check the direction in which the fibres run across the meat. Depending on which side of the animal the cut was taken from, the fibres should run diagonally from top-right to bottom-left or top-left to bottom-right.

3 Placing your knife perpendicular to the fibres, cut the meat into 4–5cm/1½–2 in steaks; you should end up with four or five steaks.

4 Pat the steaks dry on both sides and grill them on a barbecue or in a very hot grill pan until medium-rare or done to your liking. Turn the steaks on their side for 1–2 minutes, to brown and sear the fat.

5 Remove from the heat, place in a warm dish and cover. Allow to rest for 5–8 minutes.

6 Cut each steak into 1cm/½ in thick slices ensuring each slice has a trimming of fat at one end. Serve on warmed plates with any juices in the dish poured over. Serve with rice, Farofa, salsa and deep-fried polenta.

Serves 4

- 1 whole cut of beef rump cap, or picanha, about 1.25 kg/2½lb in weight
- 30ml/2 tbsp coarse sea salt
- White Rice Brazilian-style (page 84), Golden Farofa (page 94), Brazilian-style Salsa (page 96), and Deep-fried Polenta (page 88), to serve

Energy 781kcal/3288kJ; Protein 137.5g; Carbohydrate 0g, of which sugars 0g; Fat 25.6g, of which saturates 10.6g; Cholesterol 369mg; Calcium 26mg; Fibre 0g; Sodium 4305mg

Pork chops, Minas-style

Costeleta de porco à mineira

Serves 1

1 large pork chop or loin steak, about 2.5cm/1in thick

juice of ½ lime

1 clove garlic, crushed

5ml/1 tsp olive oil

salt and ground black pepper

10ml/2 tsp parsley, chopped, and lime wedges, to garnish

White Rice Brazilian-style (see page 84), Brazilian-style Shredded Greens (see page 90) and Bean Purée (see page 85), to serve

Whenever a dish is followed by the term 'à mineira', it means that it is from the state of Minas Gerais, and you can be sure it will be simple and hearty food. Here, pork chops are marinated to flavour and tenderize the meat before cooking.

1 Cut deep grooves into the fat on top of the meat, using a sharp knife. Whisk together the lime juice, garlic, olive oil and seasoning in a dish. Add the chop and rub in the marinade.

2 Set the chop aside at room temperature for up to 1 hour to allow the flavours to permeate the meat and mingle. Preheat the oven to 200°C/400°F/Gas 6.

3 Heat a griddle pan or heavy frying pan over a high heat and add the pork chop. Fry on each side for 1–2 minutes, until browned, then transfer to a shallow oven tray and bake for 10 minutes, until the fat and rind are crisp but the meat is still juicy.

4 Transfer to a warmed plate and serve with Bean Purée, rice and shredded greens.

Energy 436kcal/1820kJ; Protein 44g; Carbohydrate 0.8g, of which sugars 0.3g; Fat 28.7g, of which saturates 9.1g; Cholesterol 129mg; Calcium 35mg; Fibre 0.5g; Sodium 304mg

Black bean and pork stew

Feijoada

Feijoada is probably the best known Brazilian dish – possibly because it is the obvious menu choice when feeding a large crowd, and is often served when entertaining and at parties. A truly authentic Feijoada requires a long list of meat cuts which may be difficult to find outside Brazil or Portugal, but any pot of beans combined with chunks of pork, can be called a feijoada.

1 Put the pork ribs and the beef jerky in a large pan and cover with plenty of cold water. Bring to the boil and simmer for 45 minutes to 1 hour, replacing the water two or three times to remove the salt.

2 Drain the beef and pork. Cut the pork into separate ribs and cut the beef jerky into four or five large chunks.

3 Cut the smoked pork belly and smoked pork sausages into similar large chunks.

4 Place all the meat, together with the beans and bay leaves, in a clean pan and cover with fresh water. Bring to the boil, then lower the heat, cover, and simmer for 3–4 hours until the beans are almost cooked and the meats are soft. Top up with a little extra water, if needed, during the cooking time.

5 Heat the oil in a large frying pan and fry the onion and garlic for 10–12 minutes, stirring frequently, until they start to brown. Add to the bean and meat mixture.

6 Use some of the liquid from the beans to deglaze the frying pan and add back to the pan. Continue to simmer for a further 30 minutes, or until the meat and beans are very tender.

7 Garnish with sliced oranges and bacon lardons and serve piping hot, accompanied by rice, Farofa and polenta, and with hot pepper sauce on the side.

Cook's tips Don't let the lack of authentic ingredients dissuade you from cooking feijoada. Any sausages can be used, provided they're cooked first. You can also roast your own ribs or pork loin using a smoky barbecue marinade or a smoked paprika rub, and add them to the Feijoada. These will be softer than the cured beef jerky or smoked ribs, they won't need to be pre-boiled and should be added halfway through the beans' cooking time, not at the beginning.

When the Feijoada is ready, it can be kept on a low simmer for an hour or two, occasionally adding a little water to prevent it from drying out, so is ideal for those late arrivals.

Serves 12

300g/11oz salted smoked pork ribs

300g/11oz beef jerky

300g/11oz smoked pork belly

400g/14oz smoked pork sausages such as Portuguese paio or chouriço, or chorizo

1kg/2¼ lb dried black beans

3 bay leaves

45ml/3 tbsp vegetable oil

1 large onion, chopped

5 cloves garlic, chopped

salt

6 oranges, peeled and sliced, and deep fried bacon lardons, to garnish

White Rice Brazilian-style (page 84), Deep-fried Polenta (page 88) or Golden Farofa (page 94), Brazilian-style Shredded Greens (see page 90) and hot pepper sauce, to serve

Energy 547kcal/2305kJ; Protein 33g; Carbohydrate 63.5g, of which sugars 4.2g; Fat 20g, of which saturates 6g; Cholesterol 30mg; Calcium 95mg; Fibre 19.8g; Sodium 688mg

Side Dishes

Brazilian dinners usually consist of meat as the main focus, accompanied by a splendid variety of side dishes, ranging from seasonal vegetables and salads to deep-fried treats.

Tasty and filling accompaniments

The undisputed king of side dishes in Brazil is feijão simples (everyday black beans) eaten on its own, as an accompaniment or added to stews and casseroles. Rice is also very popular, and together with beans is cooked almost every day.

The combination of rice and beans is often enriched by the presence of Farofa (cassava flour fried in butter). Farofa is a simple side dish to prepare and each family has its own favourite recipe, which may include any number of extra elements, from bacon pieces to dried fruit and nuts. Farofa de Ovo e Banana includes fried onions, egg and banana, and is a great addition to a barbecue feast, while a dish of colourful Farofa Amarela (cassava flour toasted with palm oil) adds a wonderful nutty taste to fish dishes.

Although chips, or french fries, are now as ubiquitous as in any other country, in a true Brazilian meal they are often replaced by Batata Palha (straw-cut chips) which are deafeningly crunchy and always a big favourite with children, or Polenta Frita (deep-fried polenta). Brazilians also love salads, particularly if they contain palmito (heart of palm), a delicious delicacy extracted from young palm trees. It is a premium product but is nevertheless consumed in large quantities.

Right middle: A farmhouse in Santa Catarina, in the south of Brazil. Page 81: A stall with piles of oranges in the fruit market of Ipanema, Rio de Janeiro.

White rice Brazilian-style

Arroz branco

In Brazil, the expression, 'o arroz com feijao' (the rice and beans) means the basics or the foundation of something, reflecting that these two ingredients are staple foods. White rice is served as an accompaniment to other dishes and is also mixed with small amounts of meat or fish to make a main dish.

1 Rinse the rice in a sieve (strainer) under cold water until the water runs clear. Drain well.

2 Heat the oil in a large pan and fry the onion and garlic for 2–3 minutes until they begin to soften. Add the rice and salt, and stir for 2–3 minutes to coat the grains in the mixture. Pour in the boiling water; it should cover the rice entirely, with 1cm/½in to spare.

3 Bring the water to the boil, then lower the heat and cover the pan. Cook for 15–20 minutes, or until the grains are tender and all the water has been absorbed.

4 Remove from the heat and leave to stand, covered with the lid, for a minute or two. Stir through with a fork to separate the grains, and serve straight away.

Serves 6

- 350g/12oz/1½ cups long grain white rice
- 15ml/1 tbsp vegetable oil
- 1 small onion, finely chopped
- 1 clove garlic, finely chopped
- 600ml/1 pint/2½ cups boiling water
- 5ml/1 tsp salt

Energy 250kcal/1060kJ; Protein 4.4g; Carbohydrate 50.9g, of which sugars 0.6g; Fat 4.6g, of which saturates 0.8g; Cholesterol 0mg; Calcium 32mg; Fibre 1.7g; Sodium 330mg

Bean purée

Tutu à mineira

Serves 6

500g/1¼lb/4 cups Everyday Black Beans (see page 87)

250ml/8fl oz/1 cup water

125g/4½ oz/generous 1 cup untoasted cassava flour

30ml/2 tbsp chopped fresh parsley

3 spring onions (scallions), finely chopped

15ml/1 tbsp olive oil, plus extra, to garnish

salt

sprig of parsley, to garnish

Tutu is a traditional dish from the rural state of Minas Gerais, still cooked by local cowboys when out on a cattle drive. The dish is made with light brown beans, similar to kidney beans, but outside Minas most people use the stronger-flavoured black bean, add extra flavourings and purée the mixture rather than mash it.

1 Put the cooked black beans and water in a blender and blend for 2–3 minutes or until the mixture is a smooth purée. Pour and scrape into a medium pan.

2 Bring the bean purée to the boil, then lower the heat and gradually add the cassava flour, sprinkling only a fine dusting of it over the beans at a time.

3 Keep stirring until the mixture thickens to the consistency of a soft mash.

4 Add the chopped parsley, spring onions and olive oil and cook, stirring constantly, for 1–2 minutes. Season to taste with salt.

5 Serve hot, garnished with a drizzle of olive oil and a sprig of parsley.

Energy 184kcal/1207kJ; Protein 7.2g; Carbohydrate 34.1g, of which sugars 1.3g; Fat 3.1g, of which saturates 0.5g; Cholesterol 0mg; Calcium 43mg; Fibre 14g; Sodium 339mg

Everyday black beans

Feijão simples

Brazilians eat a whole range of beans and pulses, but the black bean is by far the most popular, and forms part of the national dish, feijoada. For many Brazilians this humble dish, Feijão – beans cooked with onions and garlic – is everyday eating. High in protein and iron, this is an excellent economical dish which can be served to supplement a small portion of meat.

Serves 6

- 350g/12oz/2 cups dried black beans
- 1 litre/1¾ pints/4 cups water
- 45ml/3 tbsp vegetable oil
- 1 onion, chopped
- 3 cloves garlic, finely chopped
- 1 bay leaf
- 5ml/1 tsp salt

1 Put the beans and water in a pressure cooker, seal the lid and cook on a high heat until steam starts to escape. Lower the heat and cook for 40 minutes, until the beans are soft. (Always follow the manufacturer's instructions when using a pressure cooker).

2 Heat the oil in a deep frying pan and fry the onion and garlic for 7–8 minutes, or until they start to brown.

3 Add a ladleful of beans and stock to the hot frying pan, and deglaze the pan by stirring together with the onion and garlic for a minute, scraping up any residue sticking to the base. Pour the mixture back into the rest of the beans in the pressure cooker.

4 Add the bay leaf to the beans, then simmer for a further 20 minutes, uncovered, until the onion is soft and the stock has reduced to a thick sauce.

5 Remove the bay leaf and stir in the salt. If you prefer a thin sauce, add in a little boiling water.

6 Serve the beans straight away while still piping hot, as an accompaniment to a rice or meat dish.

Cook's tip If you don't own a pressure cooker you will need to soak the beans overnight with enough water to cover them. The next day, drain the beans and transfer to a pan. Add 1 litre/1¾ pints/4 cups of water and simmer for 2–3 hours; top up with a little extra boiling water toward the end of cooking, if needed.

Energy 233kcal/982kJ; Protein 13.3g; Carbohydrate 27.9g, of which sugars 2.9g; Fat 8.4g, of which saturates 1.0g; Cholesterol 0mg; Calcium 65mg; Fibre 0.5g; Sodium 179mg

Deep-fried polenta

Polenta frita

Serves 6

1 litre/1¾ pints/4¼ cups water

325g/12 ½ oz/3¼ cups polenta

250ml/8fl oz/1 cup chicken stock

30ml/2 tbsp olive oil

30ml/2 tbsp plain (all-purpose) flour

vegetable oil, for deep-frying

salt

Polenta is made with ground yellow or white cornmeal. Here it is allowed to set, then deep-fried, giving it a deliciously crunchy texture. These chips can be served with all sorts of dishes, from roasted pork or chicken to stews and casseroles.

1 Pour the water into a large pan, with the polenta, stock and olive oil. Slowly bring to the boil, then simmer until it becomes a thick purée. The mixture is the correct consistency when the bottom of the pan starts to show as you stir. Sprinkle in the plain flour and continue cooking for another 3 minutes, stirring constantly.

2 Pour into an oiled 28 x 28cm/11 x 11in tin (pan), using a spatula to spread into an even layer approximately 2.5cm/1in thick. Cool, then chill in the refrigerator for 1 hour, until set.

3 Turn out the chilled block of polenta on to a lightly oiled board. Wet the blade of a knife and use it to cut into 6cm/2½ in long chips.

4 Half-fill a deep pan with oil, then heat to 190°C/375°F on a sugar thermometer. Add about a third of the chips to the oil, and fry for 3–4 minutes, until golden and crispy. Use a slotted spoon to remove them from the oil and drain on kitchen paper. Keep warm while cooking the remaining chips. Sprinkle with salt and serve straight away.

Energy 300kcal/1248kJ; Protein 5.6g; Carbohydrate 42.7g, of which sugars 0.1g; Fat 12.2g, of which saturates 1.3g; Cholesterol 0mg; Calcium 17mg; Fibre 0.2g; Sodium 161mg

Rice flour and coconut sauce

Acaçá

This is an Afro-Brazilian recipe introduced by the slaves who were transported to Brazil. Many practised the 'Candomblé' religion, in which acaçá is more than just food – it is also an offering to the gods. This dish is less of a sauce, and more a coconut-flavoured purée, which complements other Afro-Brazilian dishes.

Serves 6

30ml/2 tbsp olive oil

400ml/14fl oz/1⅔ cups coconut milk

250ml/8fl oz/1 cup milk

300g/11oz/3 cups rice flour

75ml/5 tbsp double (heavy) cream

salt and ground black pepper

1 In a large pan, mix together the olive oil, coconut milk and milk. Heat over a high heat, stirring occasionally, until it comes to the boil.

2 Turn down the heat and gradually whisk in the rice flour, sprinkling in a little at a time and stirring constantly for 5–6 minutes.

3 Stir the cream into the sauce and continue cooking for 1 minute more. Season to taste with salt and pepper and serve straight away.

Variations If you want to prepare acaçá in advance, cool, cover, then chill in the refrigerator until ready to serve. Gently reheat in a pan, with 100ml/3½fl oz/scant ½ cup milk, stirring until smooth. Acaçá sets like polenta when cool, and may also be served cold. Pour the hot sauce into a small, shallow, oiled oven tray, cover with clear film (plastic wrap) and refrigerate until set. To serve, turn out on to a cutting board and cut into diamond shapes. Garnish with coriander (cilantro) leaves.

Energy 324kcal/1350kJ; Protein 5g; Carbohydrate 45.4g, of which sugars 5.4g; Fat 13g, of which saturates 5.5g; Cholesterol 20mg; Calcium 87mg; Fibre 0g; Sodium 162mg

Brazilian-style shredded greens

Couve à mineira

Collard greens are a loose-leaf plant very similar to kale and spring greens, either of which you can use as a substitute, if necessary. Grown throughout Brazil, the leaves have a slightly bitter taste and are excellent with any rich meat dish.

1 Carefully wash each leaf and cut off most of the thick part of the stalk.

2 Stack five or six leaves on top of each other and roll tightly. Cut into very thin slices across the roll to make narrow strips of greens – the finer the better.

3 Heat the olive oil in a large, deep frying pan or wok, add the garlic and let it fry for a few seconds, then add the shredded greens. Stir for 5–6 minutes, until the greens have wilted and softened a little, but are still slightly al dente. Add salt and pepper to taste and serve straight away.

Serves 6

about 20 large leaves of spring greens (collards)

45ml/3 tbsp olive oil

4 cloves garlic, finely chopped

salt and ground black pepper

Cook's tip: At first it may look as if you have a huge amount of greens, but these lose a lot of volume and subside during cooking.

Energy 97kcal/399kJ; Protein 2.7g; Carbohydrate 2.9g, of which sugars 2.3g; Fat 8.3g, of which saturates 1.2g; Cholesterol 0mg; Calcium 175mg; Fibre 5.1g; Sodium 82mg

Deep-fried straw potatoes
Batata Palha

Serves 6

4 large potatoes, such as Maris Piper or King Edward, peeled and cut into very thin sticks

vegetable oil, for deep-frying

salt

Cook's tip To save time, use a food mandolin or a julienne disc on your food processor to cut the potatoes.

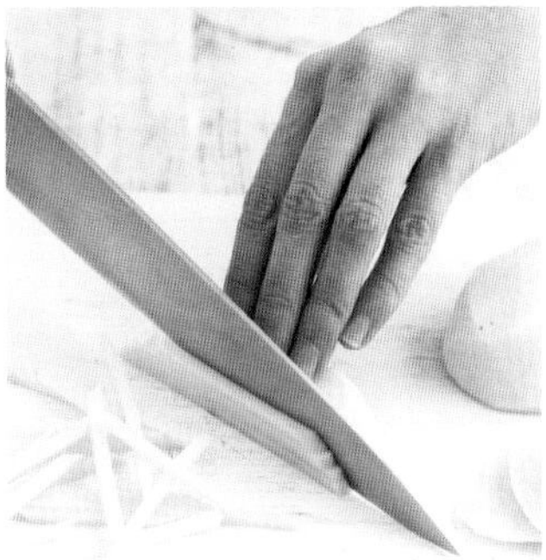

These irresistible little fried potatoes are a popular Brazilian snack as well as a main meal accompaniment. They are available in supermarkets ready-made and foil-packed, but nothing can compare to the fresh hand-made version.

1 Place the cut potato sticks in a large bowl of cold water to remove excess starch.

2 Drain well, then transfer to a large, clean, dry dish towel and pat dry. Work in batches and change the dish towel when damp.

3 Half-fill a deep-fryer or pan with oil and heat to 190°C/375°F on a sugar thermometer. Fry in batches no bigger than a large handful for 2 or 3 minutes until soft. Transfer to an oven tray and leave to cool as you fry the other batches.

4 Wait until the oil has come back up to 190°C/375°F and fry the batches a second time. This time they should puff up in volume, and become golden in colour and very crunchy.

5 Using a slotted spoon, remove from the pan and transfer to a clean oven tray covered in kitchen paper.

6 Keep warm in a moderate oven while cooking the other batches. Sprinkle with salt and serve straight away.

Energy 280kcal/1163kJ; Protein 2.8g; Carbohydrate 22.9g, of which sugars 0.8g; Fat 20.2g, of which saturates 2.3g; Cholesterol 0mg; Calcium 7mg; Fibre 2.1g; Sodium 173mg

Cassava flour egg and banana toasted in butter

Farofa de ovo e banana

If you didn't grow up with this dish, the idea of eggs, banana and something that looks like sawdust might require a culinary leap of faith. However, try it with a juicy steak or succulent grilled chicken, and you will be won over by the great combination of flavours this dish offers, with buttery toasted cassava flour and the contrasting sweetness of the banana.

Serves 6

30ml/2 tbsp vegetable oil

1 small onion, finely chopped

115g/4oz/½ cup butter

2 ripe bananas

1 large egg

400g/14oz/2⅓ cups untoasted cassava

salt

30ml/2 tbsp chopped fresh parsley, to garnish

1 Heat the oil in a deep pan or wok over a medium heat. Add the onion and fry for 7–8 minutes until soft. Add the butter to the pan and let it melt.

2 Peel the bananas and cut the flesh into 2cm/¾in slices. Add to the pan and stir for 1–2 minutes, until the edges start to soften and look translucent.

3 Beat the egg in a small bowl, until the yolk and the white are totally combined, then pour into the pan and stir to mix with the banana and onion.

4 Slowly pour the cassava flour into the banana mixture, stirring constantly. Continue to cook, for 3–4 minutes, stirring constantly, until the cassava starts to change to a light golden colour. Turn off the heat.

5 Stir in the chopped parsley, then season with salt to taste. Serve as an accompaniment to any Brazilian main dish.

Cook's tip Farofa is made from cassava (also known as manioc) flour, which has a coarse mealy texture and a delicious nutty flavour. Cassava flour can be obtained online and from specialist stores. It comes in toasted and untoasted varieties; both the farofa recipes in this chapter use the untoasted form.

Energy 317kcal/1325kJ; Protein 1g; Carbohydrate 33.2g, of which sugars 8.6g; Fat 21g, of which saturates 10.7g; Cholesterol 41mg; Calcium 20mg; Fibre 2.3g; Sodium 186mg

Golden Farofa

Farofa amarela

Serves 6

30ml/2 tbsp vegetable oil

1 onion, finely chopped

115g/4oz/½ cup butter

30ml/2 tbsp palm oil (dendê)

500g/1¼lb/5 cups untoasted cassava flour

salt

1 egg, hard-boiled and sliced, and fresh coriander (cilantro), if you wish, to garnish

This version of farofa is particularly well suited for fish dishes, especially if they are served with plenty of sauce. The farofa adds some crunch to the usual soft textures of fish, and then gradually absorbs the sauce. The rich nutty scent and deep yellow colour of the palm oil is a trademark of Afro-Brazilian cooking.

1 Heat the vegetable oil in a frying pan or a wok over a medium heat. Add the onion and fry for 7–8 minutes, until it is soft and translucent.

2 Add the butter to the pan and let it melt, then add the palm oil and mix together.

3 Add the cassava flour and stir slowly until the palm oil has coloured all the grains. Lower the heat and keep cooking for 3-4 minutes, until the farofa is golden and crunchy. Season with salt, and serve, garnished with the slices of hard-boiled egg, and coriander if you wish.

Energy 549kcal/2301kJ; Protein 2g; Carbohydrate 78.8g, of which sugars 1.5g; Fat 27.3g, of which saturates 13.3g; Cholesterol 73mg; Calcium 27mg; Fibre 0.4g; Sodium 237mg

Sautéed chayote

Xuxu refogado

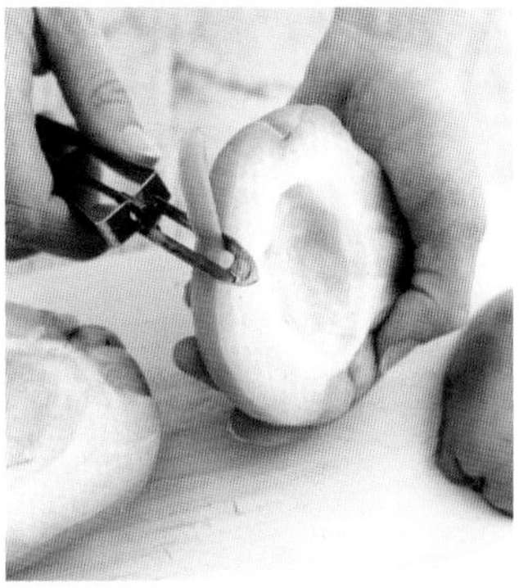

The humble xuxu, or chayote, provides a light vegetable accompaniment for any meal. Its subtle taste works best when used in conjunction with well-flavoured ingredients, such as cooked beans, meat or chicken stews. Chayote grows abundantly throughout Brazil and is sold very cheaply in most supermarkets.

Serves 6

3 chayote

30ml/2 tbsp vegetable oil

1 small onion, finely chopped

15ml/1 tbsp butter

25g/1oz/½ cup parsley, finely chopped

salt and ground black pepper

1 Cut the chayote lengthways in half and rub the two halves together under cold running water (see Cook's tip). Cut away the white core and peel the prickly outer skin. Cut into 1cm/½in dice and set aside.

2 Heat the oil in a deep frying pan and fry the onion for 7–8 minutes, until soft and translucent. Add the chayote and butter and sauté for 3 or 4 minutes until shiny and tender when pierced with the tip of a knife.

3 Stir in most of the parsley and season to taste with salt and pepper. Sprinkle with the rest of the parsley and serve straight away.

Cook's tip Some chayote have slightly sour sap in the middle, which needs to be drained away. Cutting in half, rubbing the halves together and rinsing under cold water is the easiest way to remove this. Very young chayote don't need to be peeled; if the skin is pale and tender, you can leave it on.

Energy 85kcal/353kJ; Protein 0.9g; Carbohydrate 4.6g, of which sugars 3.7g; Fat 7.2g, of which saturates 1.9g; Cholesterol 5mg; Calcium 23mg; Fibre 2.3g; Sodium 173mg

Brazilian-style salsa

Molho à campanha

This simple fresh pepper, tomato and onion salsa is a wonderful accompaniment for any grilled meat. Barbecue aficionados claim that the combination of sharp acidic flavours is a good way to cleanse your palate between different cuts of meat.

1 Chop the peppers, tomatoes and onion into 1cm/½in dice and place in a large bowl.

2 Whisk together the vinegar, oil, parsley, sugar, salt and pepper in a jug (pitcher). Pour over the chopped vegetables and stir well.

3 Serve immediately, or cover and chill in the refrigerator until you are ready to serve.

Cook's tip The flavour of the salsa improves if it stands for 15 minutes or so, but it will lose its texture if you leave it for longer than 1 hour.

Serves 6

- 1 green (bell) pepper, seeded
- 1 yellow (bell) pepper, seeded
- 3 plum tomatoes
- 1 large onion
- 100ml/3½fl oz/scant ½ cup white wine vinegar
- 200ml/7fl oz/scant 1 cup olive oil
- 25g/1oz/½ cup parsley, finely chopped
- 15ml/1 tbsp caster (superfine) sugar
- 2.5ml/½ tsp salt
- 2.5ml/½ tsp ground black pepper

Energy 346kcal/1430kJ; Protein 1.5g; Carbohydrate 9.4g, of which sugars 8.3g; Fat 33.7g, of which saturates 4.8g; Cholesterol 0mg; Calcium 23mg; Fibre 2.3g; Sodium 173mg

Palm heart salad

Salada de palmito

Serves 1–2

4 or 5 large palm heart stalks

2 ripe but firm plum tomatoes

1 large red onion

30ml/2 tbsp extra virgin olive oil

salt and ground black pepper

watercress or rocket (arugula) leaves, to garnish (optional)

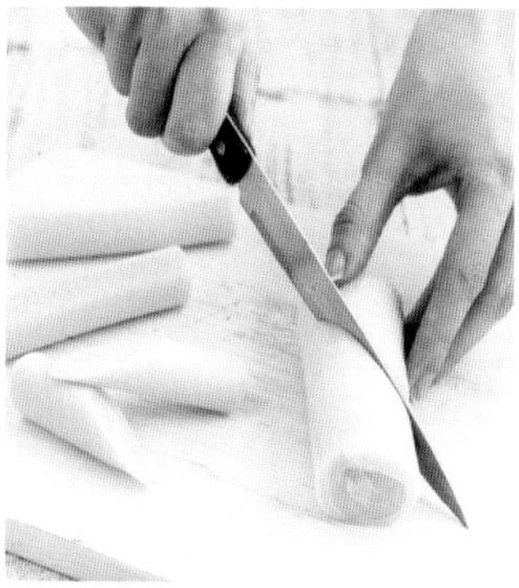

Hearts of palm (palmito) are available fresh as well as conserved in jars or canned. Fresh ones are an expensive delicacy, but most Brazilians are happy to pay a little extra for meals containing palmito, which has found its way into hundreds of recipes.

1 Trim the ends of the palm heart stalks with a sharp knife to ensure they have flat ends, then cut each in half diagonally into two equal-sized wedge shapes.

2 Cut a slice from the base of the tomato and discard. Chop the tomato into quarters.

3 Slice the onion into rings. Select a few perfect rings. Save the rest for another recipe.

4 Arrange the palm hearts and tomatoes on a serving plate, top with the onion and add a few green leaves, if you wish. Finish with a drizzle of olive oil, and salt and pepper to taste.

Energy 204kcal/843kJ; Protein 2.8g; Carbohydrate 13.6g, of which sugars 10.5g; Fat 15.7g, of which saturates 2.3g; Cholesterol 0mg; Calcium 48mg; Fibre 4.3g; Sodium 209mg

Desserts and Baking

The combination of traditional desserts with African influences, and the easy availability of sugar cane, has created a rich array of sweet cakes and desserts that Brazilians adore.

Desserts for the Brazilian sweet tooth

Baking played an important role in Brazil's colonization, as the Portuguese required cakes and other baked goods for their long expeditions, and quickly made use of local ingredients. The north of Brazil is famous for its rich cakes containing a variety of local nuts. Other common ingredients are maize – the state of Minas Gerais is famous for its Bolo de Fubá (maize cake), and of course cassava, which makes its way into every aspect of Brazilian cuisine. Bolo de Aipim (cassava cake) is a wonderfully moist cake popular in the east of Brazil, and cassava starch is the basis for Pão de Queijo, the little cheesy dough balls sold in most bakeries and snack bars throughout the country.

Coconut and egg yolk are a frequent pairing, found in a delicious tartlet known as Quindim as well as festive Beijinho de Coco (coconut drops). Maracujá (passion fruit) is one of Brazil's essential flavours, and the fresh fruit or its juice is used in numerous recipes for cakes, sweets and ice creams.

Condensed milk crops up in almost every sweet dessert or cake. Among the most famous of these recipes are Brigadeiro (chocolate truffles) and Pudim de Leite Moça (creamy caramel custard).

Right middle: Fresh coconuts ready to be sold on a beach on the Atlantic coast of Porto Seguro, Bahia.
Page 99: Sugar cane growing on one of Brazil's many plantations.

COCO
100

Coconut and egg yolk puddings

Quindim

Any pudding or cake with this many eggs in the recipe is likely to be of Portuguese origin, but the addition of coconut gives these little cakes a Caribbean flavour. They have an African name too, from the dialect spoken by the slaves brought to Brazil; quindim (pronounced 'keen-jean') means 'girlish charms' – a fitting name for these delicate little puddings. Made with just four ingredients, these tiny glistening golden treats make a wonderful dessert or can be served as a mid-morning coffee break.

Makes 12

- 12 eggs
- 225g/8oz/1 cup caster (superfine) sugar, plus extra for dusting
- 150g/5oz1 ½ cups fresh grated coconut
- 75g/3oz/generous ⅓ cup butter, melted, plus extra for greasing

Variation Desiccated unsweetened coconut may be used instead of fresh in this dish, if you prefer. The mixture can also be made in a large ring mould (like a Savarin mould), in which case it is called a quindão and served in slices.

Cook's tips Use the egg whites to make Meringue Cake (see page 115)

1 Preheat the oven to 150°C/300°F/Gas 2. Grease twelve small moulds, about 5cm/2in wide, with a generous layer of butter, then sprinkle in enough sugar to cover all the butter in a light dusting. Tip out any excess.

2 Separate the eggs, place the yolks in a fine sieve (strainer) and strain them into a large bowl. Many Brazilian cooks strain their yolks, believing it makes them silkier.

3 Add the sugar, grated coconut and melted butter to the egg yolks and mix well with a wooden spoon. Set aside for 20 minutes.

4 Stir the mixture again to combine, then divide between the moulds, filling them almost to the top with the coconut mixture.

5 Put the moulds in a roasting pan or oven dish, then pour in enough water to come halfway up the moulds. Bake for 45 minutes or until they are firm and the tops are lightly golden.

6 Remove the moulds from the hot water and leave them to cool for 10 minutes. Run a small blunt knife around the inside edges of each mould and turn the puddings out on to a large flat platter or small individual plates. Cool, then chill until ready to serve.

Cook's tip Cooking the puddings in a dish of hot water (bain marie) ensures the puddings keep their delicate texture.

Energy 254kcal/1060kJ; Protein 8.2g; Carbohydrate 138.3g, of which sugars 110.7g; Fat 9.1g, of which saturates 5.5g; Cholesterol 30mg; Calcium 384mg; Fibre 4.8g; Sodium 275mg

Coconut milk and prune pudding

Manjar

Serves 6–8

240ml/16 tbsp cornflour (cornstarch)

1 litre/1¾ pints/5 cups milk

500ml/17 fl oz/2 generous cups sweetened condensed milk

800ml/1½ pints/3 cups coconut milk

60ml/4 tbsp caster (superfine) sugar

For the syrup:

350g/12oz/1½ cups caster (superfine) sugar

250ml/8fl oz/1 cup water

120ml/4fl oz/½ cup red wine

300g/11oz stoned (pitted) ready-to-eat prunes

3 whole cloves

1 stick cinnamon

Cook's tip Manjar can also be set in little individual glasses or ramekins.

Manjar started out as a savoury soup enjoyed in the Portuguese court in the 16th century, but gradually lost its savoury elements. By the time it came to Brazil in the 19th century, the recipe was a rich dessert laced with sugar and coconut milk.

1 In a heavy pan, blend the cornflour with about 120ml/4fl oz/½ cup of the milk, then stir in the rest of the milk together with the condensed milk, coconut milk and caster sugar.

2 Put the pan over a medium heat and bring to the boil, stirring constantly. Continue stirring for 2–3 minutes, until it turns into a thick custard.

3 Rinse the inside of a 1.2–1.35 litre/2–2¼ pint/5–5½ cup mould with cold water. Pour the custard into the mould and leave to cool. Chill in the refrigerator for 3–4 hours, until set.

4 To prepare the syrup, put the caster sugar, water, wine, prunes, cloves and cinnamon in a pan over a low heat and simmer for 15 minutes or until the prunes are soft. Leave to cool.

5 Turn the set manjar out on to a deep serving plate. If this is unsuccessful, dip the mould briefly in hot water to loosen, then unmould.

6 Decorate the top with a single row of prunes and pour most of the syrup over the whole dessert. Serve cold with any remaining prunes and syrup.

Energy 954kcal/2778kJ; Protein 11g; Carbohydrate 0g, of which sugars 1g; Fat 16g, of which saturates 5g; Cholesterol 69mg; Calcium 33mg; Fibre 0.3g; Sodium 512mg

Creamy caramel custard

Pudim de leite moça

This is Brazil's answer to crème caramel, but without the richness of cream. It has a smooth, creamy texture without being too heavy and is delicious served with fresh fruit; the sharp tang of oranges and pineapples go particularly well with it.

Serves 6–8

450g/1lb/2 cups caster (superfine) sugar

30ml/2 tbsp water

400ml/14fl oz/1⅔ cups sweetened condensed milk

750ml/1¼ pints/3 cups milk

3 eggs

1 Put the sugar and water in a heavy pan. Heat gently until the sugar has dissolved, then increase the heat and boil for 7–8 minutes, until the syrup turns to a golden brown caramel, swirling the pan to ensure even browning. Immediately dip the base of the pan in cool water for a few seconds to prevent burning.

2 Pour the caramel into a 23cm/9in fluted ring mould and quickly rotate to coat the base and half-way up the sides. Leave to cool.

3 Preheat the oven to 180°C/350°F/Gas 4. Beat the eggs in a bowl with a wire whisk, then gradually whisk in the condensed milk and milk. Pour into the caramel-coated mould.

4 Alternatively, put the condensed milk, milk, and eggs in a blender for 2–3 minutes and blend until well mixed.

5 Cover the outside of the mould with foil to prevent over-browning. Place in a roasting tin or oven-proof dish. Pour in enough hot water to come halfway up the mould. Bake for 1 hour.

6 Remove the mould from the oven, allow to cool, then refrigerate for 3–4 hours, still in the mould, until completely set.

7 When you are ready to serve, carefully run a knife inside the edge of the mould to release the custard, and turn out on to a serving plate.

Energy 465kcal/1971kJ; Protein 10.3g; Carbohydrate 91.2g, of which sugars 91.2g; Fat 9.1g, of which saturates 4.9g; Cholesterol 170mg; Calcium 277mg; Fibre 0g; Sodium 145mg

Egg puffs in sugar syrup

Papo de anjo

Like several other classical Portuguese desserts based on egg yolks, Papo de Anjo is believed to have been created by Portuguese monks and nuns during the 14th or 15th centuries. Laundry was a common service performed by convents and monasteries, and their use of egg whites for starching clothes created a surplus of yolks. Brazilians call the soft area underneath your chin 'papo', so the name of this simple dessert suggests something as heavenly and light as an angel's double chin.

1 First make the syrup. Put the water, sugar, cloves and cinnamon stick in a small pan, and heat gently, stirring until the sugar dissolves.

2 Bring to the boil and simmer for 5 minutes to make a syrup. Turn off the heat and cover the pan with a lid. Leave to stand while making the egg puffs, so that the spices infuse the syrup. Preheat the oven to 160°C/325°F/Gas 3.

3 Lightly butter a 12–hole mini muffin tin (pan) or 12 small individual fixed-based tartlet tins (muffin pans), about 4cm/1½in across.

4 Whisk the whole egg and egg yolks together in a bowl until pale and fluffy and doubled in size. Carefully divide the mixture between the muffin or tartlet tins.

5 Put the tins in a roasting pan and pour in enough very hot water to come almost halfway up the tins. Bake for 30 minutes until the tops of the puffs start to brown, then remove from the oven and stand on a wire rack to cool.

6 When the tins are cool enough to handle, run a small knife around the edges of each one to remove the egg puffs.

7 Place the puffs in a serving bowl, then pour the slightly warm syrup over the top. Leave for at least 15 minutes, to allow the little puffs to soak up the syrup, before serving.

Serves 6

- 250ml/8fl oz/1 cup water
- 450g/1lb/2 cups caster (superfine) sugar
- 6 whole cloves
- 1 cinnamon stick
- unsalted butter, softened, for greasing
- 1 whole egg
- 11 egg yolks

Variation Add extra flavour to the sugar syrup by adding a couple of strips of orange zest as well as the spices. You can also add a spoonful of rum if you wish.

Cook's tip The leftover egg whites can be frozen, or used to make Guava Soufflé (see page 112).

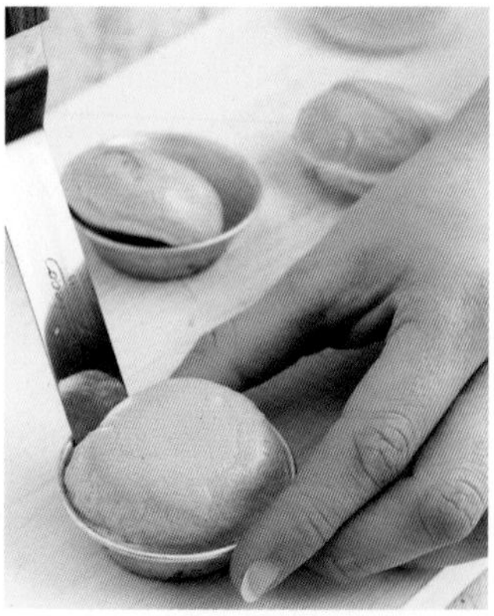

Energy 436kcal/1841kJ; Protein 6.7g; Carbohydrate 78.8g, of which sugars 78.8g; Fat 12.6g, of which saturates 4.1g; Cholesterol 416mg; Calcium 57mg; Fibre 0g; Sodium 45mg

Banana meringue pie

Torta de banana

Brazilians are banana connoisseurs, choosing from a wide variety of types available on any fruit stall to create a myriad of different dessert and main course dishes. This triple-layered dessert is a luxurious way to enjoy the very popular banana prata (silver banana), the most popular banana in Brazil; it is similar in flavour, but slightly shorter and fatter, to the Cavendish banana, the usual exported variety.

Serves 8

For the banana base:

- 565g/1lb 4½oz/generous 2½ cups caster (superfine) sugar
- 120ml/4fl oz/½ cup cold water
- 6 medium ripe bananas, cut into 2.5cm/1in thick slices

For the custard layer:

- 45ml/3 tbsp cornflour (cornstarch)
- 600ml/1 pint/2½ cups full-fat (whole) milk
- 400ml/14fl oz/1⅔ cups sweetened condensed milk
- 4 egg yolks
- 5ml/1 tsp vanilla extract
- 5ml/1 tsp butter

For the meringue topping:

- 4 egg whites
- 225g/8oz/1 cup caster (superfine) sugar
- 5ml/1 tsp grated lime zest

1 For the banana base, put the sugar and water in a heavy frying pan. Heat gently until the sugar has dissolved, then increase the heat and boil rapidly for 7–8 minutes, until the syrup turns a rich golden colour. Turn off the heat.

2 Add the banana slices to the frying pan and gently turn them while they absorb the hot caramel. The banana slices should be able to move freely in the caramel, so add a little boiling water if the mixture is too sticky.

3 Pour the banana and caramel syrup mixture into the bottom of a 23cm/9in ovenproof glass pie dish, then spread out the banana slices in an even layer. Set aside to cool.

4 For the custard, blend the cornflour with a little of the milk in a pan, then whisk in the remainder of the milk and the condensed milk. Add the egg yolks, pushing them through a fine sieve (strainer) into the pan. Stir well, then bring the mixture to the boil over a medium heat, stirring constantly, to make a thick custard.

5 As soon as the custard starts to bubble, turn off the heat and stir in the vanilla extract and butter. Pour and spread the custard evenly over the banana mixture. Preheat the oven to 220°C/425°F/Gas 7.

6 For the meringue, whisk the egg whites in a bowl until stiff. Whisk in the sugar a third at a time, whisking well between each addition until stiff and very shiny, adding the lime zest with the last of the sugar.

7 Spoon the whisked egg whites on top of the custard, piling it up in the centre and swirling with the back of the spoon or a palette knife to form peaks. Bake for 15 minutes until the top of the meringue becomes golden.

8 Serve the pie warm, or let it cool to room temperature before chilling in the refrigerator.

Cook's tip Brazilians always sieve (strain) egg yolks to remove any membrane.

Energy 722kcal/3065kJ; Protein 10.6g; Carbohydrate 157.5g, of which sugars 150.6g; Fat 9.8g, of which saturates 5.1g; Cholesterol 125mg; Calcium 263mg; Fibre 2.3g; Sodium 150mg

Avocado cream

Creme de abacate

Avocado trees are well suited to the Brazilian climate and often grow to a majestic size, producing fruit three or four times the size of avocados sold in supermarkets in the rest of the world. Their flesh is creamy, buttery and sweet, and in Brazil they feature more in sweet recipes, and are only occasionally used in savoury dishes.

1 Cut the avocado in half lengthways and remove the stone. Scoop out the flesh and chop into chunks.

2 Put the avocado, sugar, lime juice and half the milk in a blender and blend at high speed until smooth, then gradually add the remaining milk until the mixture achieves a light mousse-like consistency.

3 Once the consistency is correct, taste for sweetness, and add more sugar if needed. Spoon into individual glass bowls or tall margarita-style glasses.

Cook's tip: If not serving immediately, sprinkle lime juice over the top and cover with clear film (plastic wrap) when refrigerating, to keep the surface from going brown.

Serves 6

2 large ripe avocados

60ml/4 tbsp caster (superfine) sugar, or to taste

30ml/2 tbsp lime juice

250ml/8fl oz/1 cup milk

Energy 183kcal/761kJ; Protein 2.7g; Carbohydrate 13.8g, of which sugars 12.9g; Fat 13.4g, of which saturates 3.1g; Cholesterol 2mg; Calcium 59mg; Fibre 0g; Sodium 22mg

Papaya cream

Creme de papaya

Serves 4

2 ripe medium papaya

4 scoops vanilla ice cream

250ml/8fl oz/1 cup milk

30ml/2 tbsp crème de cassis (optional)

Cook's tip This dessert should be served as soon as it is made and eaten straight away, so prepare everything in advance and then quickly whizz it up as needed.

The papaya (pawpaw) is a delicious exotic fruit that grows wild in the lush forests of Brazil. Its juices contain an enzyme that breaks down meat fibres, so the fruit is often used as a tenderizer or eaten as an aid to digestion. It is sometimes served when still green and unripe as a vegetable, but here the ripe, sweet orange flesh is turned into one of Brazil's most popular desserts.

1 Cut the papaya in half and remove and discard the black seeds with a teaspoon. Scoop out the flesh and roughly chop.

2 Put the papaya, ice cream and the milk in a blender and purée until smooth.

3 Test the consistency, and add a little more milk if needed.

4 Serve in individual portions in glass bowls or tall margarita-style glasses, topping each with a drizzle of crème de cassis, if liked.

Energy 184kcal/770kJ; Protein 2.8g; Carbohydrate 21.3g, of which sugars 21.3g; Fat 9.2g, of which saturates 5.4g; Cholesterol 0mg; Calcium 83mg; Fibre 2.3g; Sodium 41mg

Guava soufflé

Soufflé de goiaba

Although guava is hugely popular in Brazil it is rarely eaten as a fresh fruit. Instead, it is boiled down with sugar to make a jellied guava paste, which is then dried into a solid, deep red block called 'goiabada'. The combination of a slice of goiabada and an equal-sized slice of fresh Minas cheese is Brazil's most popular dessert and is referred to as 'Romeo and Juliet'. This recipe for guava soufflé offers a less intense way of enjoying the fragrant flavour of goiabada.

Serves 6

300g/11oz goiabada, cut into chunks

30ml/2 tbsp water

6 eggs

300g/11oz/scant 1¼ cups cream cheese

250ml/8fl oz/1 cup milk

sprigs of fresh mint, to garnish

1 Preheat the oven to 120°C/250°F/Gas ½. Put the goiabada and water in a small pan and gently heat until completely melted, stirring occasionally. Turn off the heat.

2 Separate the eggs and whisk the whites together, in a large bowl, until stiff peaks form.

3 Stir a spoonful of the egg whites into the melted guava mixture to loosen it a little, then pour the melted guava into the egg whites and gently fold in.

4 Spoon the mixture into six 150ml/¼ pint/⅔ cup deep ramekins, then run a knife around the inside wall of the ramekins, which will help the soufflés to rise.

5 Place on an oven tray on the middle oven shelf, then turn up the oven temperature to 180°C/350°F/Gas 4 and bake for 15 minutes.

6 Meanwhile, gently heat the cream cheese and the milk together a small pan, stirring occasionally until the cream cheese has melted. Pour into a small jug or bowl and leave to cool slightly.

7 Garnish each souffle with a small sprig of fresh mint and serve straight away with the melted cream cheese.

Cook's tip If you find it difficult to find goiabada, this recipe also works well with Spanish membrillo or quince preserve.

Energy 341kcal/1414kJ; Protein 11.1g; Carbohydrate 4.5g, of which sugars 4.4g; Fat 31.2g, of which saturates 17.2g; Cholesterol 282mg; Calcium 141mg; Fibre 2.4g; Sodium 256mg

Meringue cake

Pudim de clara

This simple meringue cake looks spectacular, even though it is very easy to make, and is usually served at parties and social gatherings. It is perfect when you've got a surplus of egg whites, and so is often made at the same time as desserts that use only yolks, such as Quindim or Papo de Anjo.

Serves 8

For the caramel:

225g/8oz/1 cup caster (superfine) sugar

120ml/4fl oz/½ cup water

For the cake:

6 egg whites

180ml/12 tbsp caster sugar

2.5ml/½ tsp lime zest

2.5ml/½ tsp vanilla extract

2.5ml/½ tsp cream of tartar

Cook's tip Give your Pudim de Clara an extra Brazilian twist by drizzling some fresh passion fruit pulp over it, seeds and all. The tart taste and strong perfume of the passion fruit helps cut through the sweetness of the caramel.

1 Put the sugar and water in a heavy pan. Heat gently until the sugar has dissolved, then increase the heat and boil rapidly for 7–8 minutes, until the syrup turns into a rich golden brown caramel. Keep swirling the pan as it boils to ensure even browning.

2 As soon as the syrup turns to caramel, immediately dip the base of the pan in cool water for a few seconds to prevent further cooking. Then pour into a 23cm/9in ring mould and quickly rotate it to coat the sides with caramel. Leave to cool.

3 Preheat the oven to 160°C/325°F/Gas 3. For the cake, whisk the egg whites in a bowl until soft peaks form. Whisk in a third of the sugar, then whisk in a second third of the sugar until stiff and very shiny.

4 Add the last of the sugar to the eggs, together with the lime zest, vanilla extract and cream of tartar, and whisk again to combine. Use a spoon or a spatula to transfer the meringue to the ring mould, spreading evenly.

5 Bang the mould down on the work surface to compact the mixture and ensure there are no gaps or large air holes inside.

6 Bake the cake on the middle shelf of the oven for 30 minutes, until golden. Turn off the oven but leave the cake inside for 10 minutes with the door half open – this will prevent the meringue from sinking.

7 Carefully turn the cake out on to a deep cake dish. Leave to cool, then chill before serving.

Energy 208kcal/887kJ; Protein 2.2g; Carbohydrate 53.2g, of which sugars 53.2g; Fat 0g, of which saturates 0g; Cholesterol 10mg; Calcium 6mg; Fibre 0g; Sodium 48mg

Hominy corn porridge

Mugunzá

Serves 8

250g/9oz/1½ cups hominy corn

115g/4oz/½ cup caster (superfine) sugar

400ml/14fl oz/1⅔ cups coconut milk

5ml/1 tsp salt, or to taste

4 whole cloves

2 sticks cinnamon

250ml/8fl oz/1 cup milk (optional)

To serve:

15ml/1 tbsp ground cinnamon

115g/4 oz/⅔ cups raw peanuts, chopped

8 sticks cinnamon (optional)

Mugunzá is made from hominy, a bleached corn (maize) product, originally from Central America. Adopted by the Candomblé religion, still practised by African descendants in Brazil, hominy is used as an offering to their gods. Mugunzá is enjoyed during winter, and in the southern states, where it is known as 'cangica'.

1 Put the hominy in a bowl, cover with cold water, and leave to soak for at least 8 hours, or overnight, if preferred. Drain well, then tip into a large pan and pour over enough water to cover. Bring to the boil, reduce the heat, cover, and simmer for 1 hour, until tender. Drain again.

2 Return to the pan and add the sugar, coconut milk, salt, cloves and cinnamon sticks. Simmer for 40–60 minutes, stirring occasionally, especially near the end of the cooking time.

3 Add extra milk, if needed, during cooking, to keep the mixture from becoming too thick.

4 Serve the porridge hot, in bowls, garnished with a sprinkling of cinnamon, chopped peanuts, and a stick of cinnamon if liked.

Cook's tip Hominy is corn that has been treated with an alkali. It can be bought as whole kernels or ground. Outside the Americas, it can be bought at specialist food shops or online.

192kcal/812kJ; Protein 4.1g; Carbohydrate 41.4g, of which sugars 19g; Fat 1.9g, of which saturates 0.4g; Cholesterol 2mg; Calcium 59mg; Fibre 0g; Sodium 315mg

Maize cake

Bolo de fubá

Fubá is a very fine milled maize flour, a delicate cousin of polenta. It is widely used throughout Brazil, especially in the state of Minas Gerais, to make a number of different breads and cakes, but this is perhaps the simplest of all. A small amount of hard cheese gives the cake a fantastic savoury and salty depth.

1 Preheat the oven to 190°C/375°F/Gas 5. Grease and flour the sides of a 20cm/8in springform cake tin (pan), and line the base with baking parchment.

2 In a large bowl, cream the butter and sugar together until light and fluffy. Separate the eggs and add the yolks one at a time to the mixture, ensuring each is fully incorporated before you mix in the next one.

3 Add the fubá and the cheese and aniseed (if using) to the bowl, and beat for another minute.

4 In a separate bowl, whisk the egg whites until stiff peaks form, then gently fold them into the yolk and sugar mixture. Sift the self-raising flour over the mixture and fold it in carefully with a metal spoon.

5 Spoon the cake mixture into the prepared tin and smooth the surface level. Bake for 30–40 minutes, until the cake is firm to the touch.

6 Remove the cake from the oven and allow to stand in the tin for 10 minutes before turning out on to a wire rack. Serve while still warm.

Serves 12

225g/8oz/1 cup butter, softened

225g/8oz/1 cup caster (superfine) sugar

4 eggs

125g/4¼ oz/generous 1 cup fubá (fine maize flour)

45ml/3 tbsp queijo curado or Parmesan cheese, finely grated (optional)

5ml/1 tsp ground aniseed (optional)

125g/4½oz/generous 1 cup self-raising (self-rising) flour

Cook's tip This cake is best enjoyed while still slightly warm, and is especially good served with small cups of espresso coffee.

Energy 332kcal/1358kJ; Protein 6g; Carbohydrate 35.3g, of which sugars 20; Fat 19.2g, of which saturates 1.1g; Cholesterol 121mg; Calcium 92mg; Fibre 0.9g; Sodium 209mg

Rolled sponge cake with guava filling

Rocambole de goiabada

A truly international concoction, this recipe has a French name, a Portuguese sponge and a very Brazilian filling. Rocambole is a rolled cake made with pão de ló, an egg-rich cake mixture made with no butter, which gives it a very light and springy texture. Goiabada – guava preserve – is the most popular filling, with doce de leite (dulce de leche) a close second, but any type of jam can be used.

Serves 8

For the sponge:

- 8 eggs, separated
- 80g/3oz/scant ⅔ cup caster (superfine) sugar
- 75g/2¾oz/generous ½ cup self raising (self-rising) flour

For the filling:

- 250g/9oz jam, goiabada or dulce de leche
- 60ml/4 tbsp water
- 45ml/3 tbsp caster (superfine) sugar, for sprinkling

Cook's tip It is important to trim off the long sides or the sponge will be difficult to roll and may crack.

1 Line the base and short sides of a shallow 38x30cm/15x12in cake tin (pan) with a single strip of baking parchment. The two long sides of the tin should be buttered and then dusted with flour.

2 If using goiabada for the filling, cut into small chunks, and place in a small pan with the water. Gently heat the goiabada, stirring occasionally, until completely melted. Set aside. Preheat the oven to 180°C/350°F/Gas 4.

3 In a large bowl, whisk the egg yolks and sugar together until they are pale and thick.

4 In a separate bowl whisk the egg whites until stiff peaks form. Fold into the yolk mixture, then sift the flour over the mixture and gently fold in.

5 Transfer the cake mixture to the prepared tin and bake for 25 minutes, or until it turns a very light brown and springs back when lightly pressed. Remove from the oven and let it cool in the tin for 10 minutes.

6 Lay a clean dish towel on the worktop and sprinkle with caster sugar. Turn out the sponge on to the towel. Trim 1cm/½ in of cake off the two long edges.

7 Spread the melted goiabada, or other filling, over the sponge in a thin layer. Hold one end of the towel with both hands and use it to roll the cake from one of the short sides to the other.

8 Transfer to a serving plate, seam-side down, dust with sugar and serve. It is delicious with whipped cream or crème fraiche.

Energy 118kcal/794kJ; Protein 8.8g; Carbohydrate 24.6g, of which sugars 18.1g; Fat 6.8g, of which saturates 1.9g; Cholesterol 232mg; Calcium 72mg; Fibre 1.8g; Sodium 119mg

Potato buns

Pão de batata

Fill one of these with a couple of slices of good ham and some plain Minas cheese and you'll be instantly transported to a colonial farmhouse in the country with chickens in the front yard. The rolls are also perfect for serving with soup.

1 Put the yeast, sugar, salt, milk and vegetable oil in a large bowl and whisk together well.

2 Add the potato and the beaten egg to the bowl, and stir well with a sturdy spoon or spatula to mix all the ingredients.

3 Gradually sift the flour over the mixture and work it in with your hand. Stop adding flour when the mixture stops sticking to your hand; the less you add, the lighter the buns will be.

4 Transfer the dough to a floured surface and knead for 5–8 minutes, until smooth. Add a few more dustings of flour if needed, but do not exceed the quantity given in the recipe.

5 Form the dough into a sausage shape and cut into about 24 pieces.

6 Grease and flour two baking sheets. Using the palms of your hand, roll the pieces of dough into balls and place them, evenly spaced, on the baking sheets. Cover with a slightly damp cloth and set aside in a warm draught-free place to rest and rise for 1 hour.

7 Preheat the oven to 190°C/375°F/Gas 5. Bake the buns for 20–30 minutes, until the tops are golden and the buns are cooked. Remove from the oven and leave them to cool on the trays for 5–10 minutes, before serving with some good butter or creamy cheese.

Makes about 24 buns

15g/½oz packet easy-blend (rapid-rise) dried yeast

15ml/1 tbsp caster (superfine) sugar

15ml/1 tbsp salt

150ml/¼ pint/⅔ cup warm milk

30ml/2 tbsp vegetable oil

350g/12oz/1 cup mashed potato (cooled and pushed through a ricer)

1 egg, beaten

about 400g/14oz/4 cups plain (all-purpose) flour

Energy 83kcal/352kJ; Protein 2.6g; Carbohydrate 16.4g, of which sugars 1.3g; Fat 1.2g, of which saturates 0.3g; Cholesterol 10mg; Calcium 34mg; Fibre 0.9g; Sodium 90mg

Cheesy dough balls

Pão de queijo

Makes about 24 balls

500g/1¼lb/5 cups sour cassava starch (polvilho azedo)

20ml/4 tsp salt

450ml/¾ pint/2 cups milk

250ml/8fl oz/1 cup vegetable oil

225g/8oz/1 cup feta cheese, finely crumbled

100g/4oz/1 cup Parmesan cheese, grated

4 eggs

cream cheese or butter, to serve

Cook's tip Sour cassava starch, also known as sour tapioca, can be bought online or from specialist stores.

Variation You can freeze the rolls before cooking, and bake directly from frozen.

These little golden dough balls are another great example of the versatility of cassava as a cooking ingredient. Pão de queijo can be found in the majority of bakeries, snack bars, grill houses and restaurants in Brazil.

1 Preheat the oven to 200°C/400°F/Gas 6. Carefully put the sour starch into a bowl; it is very fine and easily blows away. Add the salt.

2 Heat the milk and oil in a pan until it reaches boiling point. Just as the boiling liquid starts to rise, remove from the heat and pour it over the sour starch, mixing well with a wooden spoon. Keep mixing until the starch and liquid clump together in a texture similar to scrambled eggs. Set aside to cool.

3 Once the starch mixture has cooled down completely, add the feta and Parmesan cheeses and eggs. Use a mixer with a bread hook, or use your hands to mix.

4 Mix or squeeze the dough until all the ingredients have come together; the dough will get firmer as you mix it.

5 Grease the palm of your hands with a dab of oil. Take a small piece of dough, and roll it in your your palms to form a ball. Repeat until all the mixture is used up. Place the balls on an ungreased baking sheet as you go.

6 Bake on the top shelf of the oven for 15 minutes. Reduce the temperature to 150°C/300°F/Gas 2 and bake for a further 10–15 minutes or until lightly browned and cooked. Serve warm, accompanied with some cream cheese or good butter.

Energy 232kcal/967kJ; Protein 5g; Carbohydrate 20.2g, of which sugars 1.1g; Fat 15.1g, of which saturates 3.8g; Cholesterol 50mg; Calcium 108mg; Fibre 0g; Sodium 527mg

Cassava cake

Bolo de aipim

Serves 12

- 20g/¾oz/1½ tbsp butter, softened
- 450g/1lb/2 cups caster (superfine) sugar
- 4 eggs, separated
- 100g/4oz/1 cup grated fresh coconut
- 300g/11oz cassava root, finely grated
- 250ml/8fl oz/1 cup milk
- 175g/6oz/1½ cups self-raising (self-rising) flour

This cake's rich flavour and fluffy texture is made even lighter with the addition of whisked egg whites, and it contains little fat. It is popular at carnivals held in June in the north of Brazil. The ubiquitous cassava root gives the cake a lovely moist texture.

1 Preheat the oven to 190°C/375°F/Gas 5. Grease and line the base of a 23cm/9in square cake tin (pan) with baking parchment.

2 In a large bowl, beat the butter and sugar together until the mixture looks crumbly. Add the yolks one by one, ensuring each is well incorporated before adding the next one.

3 Beat the egg mixture for 3–4 minutes, then add the grated coconut, cassava and milk and mix to combine.

4 Sift the flour into the bowl, and with a metal spoon, gently fold it in to the egg mixture.

5 In a separate bowl, whisk the egg whites into stiff peaks, then add to the egg yolk and cassava mixture and carefully fold in.

6 Spoon the cake mixture into the prepared tin and bake for 40 minutes, or until golden-brown and firm. Remove from the oven and leave in the tin for 10 minutes before turning out and cooling on a wire rack.

Energy 357kcal/1523kJ; Protein 4.5g; Carbohydrate 73.9g, of which sugars 40.1g; Fat 6.8g, of which saturates 4.1g; Cholesterol 81mg; Calcium 77mg; Fibre 2.3g; Sodium 94mg

Peanut brittle

Pé de moleque

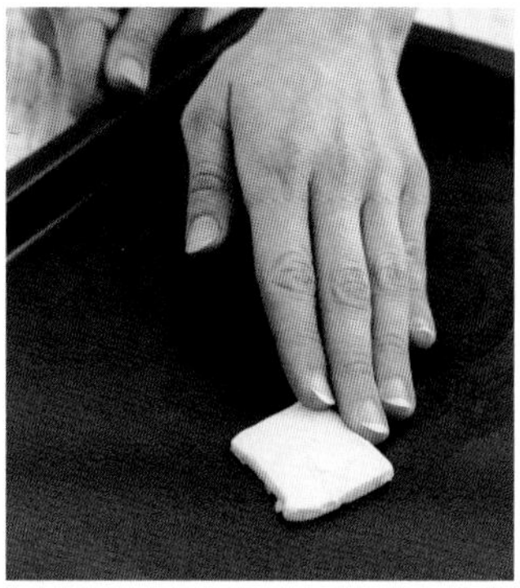

Makes about 30 pieces

- 250ml/8fl oz/1 cup golden (light corn) syrup
- 450g/1lb/2 cups caster (superfine) sugar
- 350g/12oz/3 cups raw peanuts
- 10ml/2 tsp bicarbonate of soda (baking soda)
- 15ml/1 tbsp butter

Cook's tip: Serve the brittle on the same day or keep in a cool place in an airtight container. Store in a single layer if possible and bear in mind that humidity will make the brittle sticky.

This delicious toffee's name translates as 'poor boy's foot'. In colonial Brazil, roads were made with loose stones in a layer of sand. Street boys were employed to stomp on them to flatten the surface, and they came to be called 'pé de moleque'.

1 Grease a baking sheet or marble surface with butter. In a large pan, heat the golden syrup, sugar and peanuts and stir over a low heat, until the sugar has dissolved.

2 Turn the heat up and continue to cook, until the mixture becomes a golden caramel colour and you can hear the peanuts pop. Lower the heat and cook for 3–4 minutes.

3 Add the bicarbonate of soda and beat vigorously with a wooden spoon. Remove from the heat and continue mixing for 30 seconds.

4 Pour on to the buttered baking sheet and use a knife to spread the mixture to 1cm/½ in thick. Wait 5 minutes, then use a sharp knife and a ruler (or the edge of an oven tray) to score the surface of the mixture with criss-cross lines, making diamonds of about 2.5x5cm/1x2in.

5 When the mixture is cooled but not totally cold, cut along the score lines with a heavy knife to make the diamond shapes. You may need to hit the back of the knife with a rolling pin to help crack the mixture. Alternatively, crack the brittle into rough pieces when cold.

Energy 153kcal/646kJ; Protein 3g; Carbohydrate 23.8g, of which sugars 23.1g; Fat 5.8g, of which saturates 1.3g; Cholesterol 1mg; Calcium 10mg; Fibre 0.9g; Sodium 118mg

Chocolate truffles

Brigadeiro

These chocolate treats, named after Brigadier Eduardo Gomes of the Brazilian Air Force, are an absolute must for any child's party in Brazil, but are equally popular with the grown-ups. This simple recipe is a fun one to make as a group activity.

1 Heat the condensed milk, butter and chocolate powder in a pan over a medium heat.

2 Simmer for about 20 minutes, stirring constantly, until it reaches a very dense and fudgy consistency. You should be able to see the bottom of the pan when you scrape it with your spoon. Turn down the heat a little toward the end of cooking, to prevent it from burning.

3 Transfer the mixture to a bowl and leave it to cool at room temperature, then place it in the refrigerator for 30 minutes, or until very firm.

4 Pour the chocolate sprinkles into a shallow bowl. Grease the palms of your hands with a thin layer of butter. Scoop out a spoonful of the mixture at a time and roll to form a ball.

5 Drop each truffle ball into the bowl with chocolate sprinkles and use a fork to push it around until it is totally coated in sprinkles. Place the ball in a mini paper case, and repeat until all the truffle mixture has been used up.

6 Serve, arranged on a serving plate, and accompanied by beijinhos de coco (opposite).

Makes 25–30

- 400g/14oz can sweetened condensed milk
- 15ml/1 tbsp butter
- 45ml/3 tbsp drinking chocolate powder
- 100g/4oz/1 cup chocolate sprinkles

Cook's tip Try rolling your Brigadeiros in other finishings like coloured sugar sprinkles, coconut, chopped nuts or just sugar. Serious chocoholics should use unsweetened cocoa powder instead of drinking chocolate and roll them in finely grated dark (bittersweet) chocolate or more cocoa powder.

Energy 72kcal/303kJ; Protein 1.4g; Carbohydrate 10.5g, of which sugars 10.4g; Fat 3g, of which saturates 2.1g; Cholesterol 6mg; Calcium 39mg; Fibre 0g; Sodium 29mg

Coconut drops

Beijinho de coco

Makes about 60

225g/8oz/1 cup caster (superfine) sugar

120ml/4fl oz/½ cup milk

7g/½ tbsp butter

175g/6oz/1½ cups fresh grated coconut

120ml/4fl oz/½ cup orange juice

5ml/1 tsp finely grated orange rind

2.5ml/½ tsp finely grated lime rind

1 egg yolk, lightly beaten

2.5ml/½ tsp vanilla extract

caster (superfine) sugar, for rolling

whole cloves, to decorate (optional)

Beijinhos de coco are the perfect partners for Brigadeiros and one is hardly ever seen far from the other. The name means 'little coconut kisses' and if you get the job of handing them round you will always be the most popular person at the party!

1 Mix the sugar, milk and butter together in a pan and bring to a boil. Simmer for a further 15 minutes, stirring constantly.

2 Remove from the heat and add the coconut, orange juice, and the orange and lime rind. Mix briefly, then add the egg yolk and stir well.

3 Return the pan to the heat and stir constantly until the mixture has thickened enough to show the bottom of the pan when stirring.

4 Remove the pan from the heat, stir in the vanilla extract and leave until completely cold.

5 Spread the caster sugar on a plate or dish. Scoop up teaspoonfuls of the mixture, then roll into balls in the sugar. Keep rolling until completely coated, decorate each with a clove, if using, and place in a paper case.

6 Arrange on a serving plate, or dish, together with Brigadeiros (see opposite).

Energy 29kcal/120kJ; Protein 0.22g; Carbohydrate 4.3g, sugars 4.3g; Fat 13g, of which saturates 1g; Cholesterol 4mg; Calcium 4mg; Fibre 0.4g; Sodium 3mg

Suppliers

UK

Brazil Express
(Açaí bar and food store selling coffee, groceries, snacks and pastries)
Stratford Shopping Centre
Unit 10, 70–73 The Mall
London E15 1XQ
Tel: 020 8221 2524
www.brazilexpress.co.uk

Bermondsey Brazilian Shop
(Brazilian groceries)
250 Jamaica Road
London SE16 4BD
Tel: 020 7237 1220
www.londonbbs.com

Boi Gordo Butchers
(Fresh meat and grocery)
125 Greengate Street
London E13 0BG
Tel: 07454 680127

Supermercado Portugal
(Online Brazilian and Portuguese groceries and cured meats)
Unit 1 Canary Way
Norwich
NR1 1WY
www.supermercadoportugal.com

Bem Brasil
(Churrascaria restaurants)
Manchester Tel: 0161 893 2525
Liverpool Tel: 0151 709 0044
www.bembrasilrestaurants.com

Rodizio Rico
207 Wharfside
Birmingham B30 3LH
Tel: 0121 285 2856
www.rodiziorico.com

EUROPE

Favela Chic, Paris
(Brazilian restaurant)
Tel: 01 40 21 38 14
www.favelachic.com

Gabriela, Paris
Tel: 01 42 80 28 14
www.gabriela.fr

El Novilla Carioca
(Churrascaria restaurant)
Mozart, 7, Madrid 28008, Spain
Tel: 915 485 140
www.novillocarioca.com

Sucos Do Brasil
Mühlenstrasse 10
40213 Düsseldorf, Germany
Tel: 49 211 132 650

USA

Emporium Brasil
15 W. 46th Street
New York, NY 10036
Tel: (212) 764 4646
www.emporiumbrasil.com

Búzios
Brazilian market
8th Floor
17–19 W 45th Street
New York NY 10036
Tel: (212) 869 6552
www.buziosnyc.com

El Mercado Meat Market
(Brazilian cured meat)
3767 N. Southport Avenue
Chicago, IL 60613
Tel: (773) 477 5020
www.folklorechicago/El_mercado

Via Brasil
(Brazilian groceries and meat)
15400 Biscayen Blvd 102
North Miami, Florida
Tel: (786) (55 6159
www.viabrasil.com

BrazilMart grocery store
2107 SW 27th Avenue

Miami FL 33145
Tel: (305) 857 0885
www.brazilmart.com

Brazilian Bakery Cafe
1260 Powers Ferry Road
Marietta GA 30067
Tel: (770) 818 0088
www.brazilianbakery.com

Padara Brasil
(Bakery)
125 Harvard Avenue
Boston MA 02134
Tel: (617) 202 6783

Samba Taste of Brazil
(Restaurant, café, groceries)
922 Main Street
Hoopkins MN 55343
Tel: (952) 935 2708

Index